TRENDS IN BANK CREDIT AND FINANCE

TRENDS IN BANK CREDIT AND FINANCE

Lectures delivered at

THE THIRTEENTH INTERNATIONAL BANKING SUMMER SCHOOL

NOORDWIJK

SEPTEMBER 1960

SPRINGER-SCIENCE+BUSINESS MEDIA, B.V.

ISBN 978-94-011-8736-7 ISBN 978-94-011-9588-1 (eBook)
DOI 10.1007/978-94-011-9588-1

CONTENTS

Opening Address

DELIVERED BY TJ. GREIDANUS
Chairman of the Nederlandse Bankiersvereniging
Partner Messrs. Pierson, Heldring & Pierson

On behalf of the Netherlands Bankers Association and the Comité de Patronage it is a real pleasure to me to welcome you all here as participants in the International Banking Summer School.

It has been a great privilege for our Association to organize the Banking Summer School this year and we are delighted to welcome here so many representatives from other countries, who we hope and expect will before long occupy leading positions in the banking profession. You are the bankers of the future and as such you will have to bear great responsibilities. Any manager in any sort of business carries a great responsibility, but for the banker there is the added responsibility for monetary equilibrium.

It is not necessary, here, for me to stress the paramount importance of monetary equilibrium for the regular and most efficient development of the world's resources and for a just distribution of manufactured products.

In my opinion, there are four widely differing factors which have a significant part to play in achieving and preserving monetary equilibrium.

In the first place we have the governments, which exert an exceptionally strong influence through their budgetary policy and the way in which state expenditure is financed.

Secondly, we have the central banks, which are immediately responsible for the maintenance of monetary equilibrium, and also the private banks which work in close cooperation with them.

Thirdly, there are those authorities which direct wage policies and which exert their influence on the level of wages in relation to productivity.

Finally, monetary equilibrium in the present monetary system is in many countries dependent on that in other countries, since their currencies are interdependent as a result of maintained exchange rates.

As regards the responsibility of categories I and III, Government and Trade Unions, we need not concern ourselves here. Let us look at our own task in this respect.

As regards the fourth category – the influence of foreign countries on monetary equilibrium in our own country – there is in my opinion only one solution. The influence exerted by other countries is a consequence of the interdependence which results from the system of more or less fixed rates of exchange between the various currencies. The only solution will be to make that interdependence still closer, eventually by the creation of central banks for groups of countries and ultimately of one central bank for all the countries that maintain the same monetary system. Such a central bank should be charged with the control of credits, governmental as well as credits to trade and industry in the various countries under its jurisdiction. Needless to say, this must be wishful thinking for the time being, and the creation of such a centralized system is still far off.

Let us therefore look at the role of central banks and private banks in connection with monetary equilibrium.

Many years ago economists argued whether private banks could create money by granting credits or whether they could only grant credits from their own cash balances. We can now assume that the general opinion, to put it simply, is that "loans create deposits" and that therefore private banks can create money and often do.

Nevertheless I have always held the opinion that in their assumption that private banks create money economists have gone too far. No attention, or at least not sufficient attention, has been given to the still more important question whether private banks are free to create money or whether they are limited in this respect and if so in what way.

As long ago as 1932, I discussed this subject in my book on *The Value of Money*, notably in Chapter XXVI, which dealt with private banks. My theory regarding this problem is based on the fact that both deposit money and bank notes have their own functions as media of exchange. Deposit money is needed in particular for the wholesale trade and large transactions, but is less suitable when money is needed for smaller transactions. Thus there is a demand by the public for deposit money on the one hand and for bank notes on the other; the relation between these two is determined by the demand of the public.

The private banks cannot create too much deposit money because then the public will ask for bank notes to restore the equilibrium, and want to cash part of their credit balances. On the other hand, when the circulation of bank notes becomes too large in comparison with deposit money, bank notes will flow to the private banks. Thus the relation between the two can be disturbed only temporarily.

If, therefore, the central bank reduces the amount of bank notes in circulation, the relation between bank notes and deposit money is disturbed and the public will withdraw part of their credit balances. The possibility of the creation of deposit money by the private banks is accordingly limited. For it is the public which determines the relation between deposit money and bank notes.

Is it possible to have this theory confirmed?

It is unfortunate that in the science of economics we cannot avail ourselves of laboratories to prove our theories. However, in this particular instance we have had an experience in this country which has enabled us to confirm the correctness of this theory. And, the theory having been confirmed, we can draw conclusions from temporary deviations in the relation between deposit money and bank notes which can be helpful for the efficient management of the currency.

The experience to which I referred was gained after the second world war, when in September 1945 in the Netherlands all bank notes were withdrawn from circulation. At the same time all credit balances in the private banks were blocked. Every citizen received ten guilders in cash for his needs in the first week, and thereafter new earnings could be spent as so-called "free money." At the end of the year 1938 the percentage of bank notes to deposit money and bank notes together was 41.2 and it had been about the same for a number of years. The money purge in September 1945 caused a revolution in the monetary system, but by the end of October 1945 we could again speak of a new relation being established. The percentage of bank notes was then 30.9. In November 1945 bank notes were 30.6% of the total; in December 1945 34.9%. At the end of the year 1946 bank notes had even surpassed the pre-war percentage, namely 45.2%; at the end of 1947 the percentage had dropped again to 44.0; by the end of 1948 to 43.4; and by 1949 the old relation had been restored with 41.4% in the form of bank notes. This relation was more or less maintained for the next few years, with the exception of the year 1951, when, probably as a result of the Korean crisis, bank notes went up to nearly 44%. At the end of 1952, however, the percentage was again down to 41.6. Then in 1956, when there was a weak tendency for guilders and a few other European currencies, the percentage went up to 45.7 and in 1957 it rose to as much as 48.2. After that, bank notes reacted again to 45.3% at the end of 1958 and to 44.3% at the end of 1959.

We can thus see that the theory has been proved by the facts after the money purge in that, through the relation between deposit money and bank notes established by the demand of the public, the creation of deposit money is more or less automatically linked to the creation of bank notes.

This means that in normal conditions the central bank, when controlling the issue of bank notes, at the same time controls the creation of deposit money by the private banks. However, normal conditions do not always prevail. Apart from wages policy, which I shall not treat here, I have already mentioned governmental budgetary policies and the impact on our own currency of monetary conditions abroad. In this connection it is the task of the private banks to co-operate with the central bank in the control of the currency. This co-operation may be needed in the case of too large floating debts of the State and local authorities.

It may also be needed if monetary equilibrium is endangered when gold and foreign exchange is flowing to a country, but the role played by private banks in this respect can easily be misunderstood and I therefore want to dwell a little on this subject.

When a higher rate can be obtained in a foreign money market than at home, the private banks will buy foreign exchange for cash and sell forward against it. In our country this has of late been the case, for example with dollars, and for the sake of simplicity I shall limit myself here to dollars. Such a swap means that the banks borrow the dollars from residents and lend guilders to them. They credit their customers and by this means they create deposit money. In the same way as credits, swaps also create deposits.

The dollars they borrow and which were at the disposal of their counterparts before the swap are now invested by the banks. In this way they grant credits abroad in place of their counterparts.

At home they give a credit to the other party in the swap with exactly the same consequences for monetary equilibrium as in the case of any other form of granting of credit.

As soon as the granting of other credits becomes more profitable, or when the rate of interest in the United States plus a premium or minus a discount for the swap becomes less attractive, the banks will withdraw their dollars and let their swaps expire.

In the first case, when other credits are in demand by customers of the banks, there is no increase in the granting of credits to the private sector, but only a replacement.

In the second case, when there is no demand for credit in a form other than the swap, the counterparts will again be debited on the due date of the forward dollars. By this contraction of credit the deposit money will be wiped out and have a deflationary effect.

It is possible that the forward dollars which have then become cash dollars are sold to De Nederlandsche Bank, and the deposit money is thus replaced by bank notes or credit balances with the central bank.

When the banks buy cash dollars (for instance, the proceeds of Dutch shares sold in the United States) then of course there is no granting of credits, but nevertheless deposit money is created. The consequences for monetary equilibrium are the same as in the case of credit expansion. As a result of the close relation between the quantity of bank notes in circulation and the quantity of the credit balances in the banks the effect on monetary equilibrium is eventually the same whether the foreign exchange is bought by the private banks or by the central bank.

What happens when dollars originally bought by the private banks are sold to the central bank?

The deposit money was already created when the banks bought the dollars and the percentage of bank notes in comparison with deposit money was then reduced. By the sale of the dollars to the central bank deposit money is again comparatively reduced. The same result is then reached as would have been the case if the dollars had been sold immediately to the central bank. In both cases deposit money is created immediately. The influence on monetary equilibrium of an offer of foreign exchange is always felt immediately.

In normal conditions the central bank can control the issue of bank notes by methods other than changes in the official rate of discount. Open market policy is a second means. Through the relatively steady relation between the quantity of bank notes and of deposit money, the central bank at the same time controls the creation of deposit money.

However, when there is too much liquidity in the country, either as a consequence of public finances or of the inflow of gold and foreign exchange, then there is a task for private banking to co-operate with the central bank in the management of the currency. In some situations they will even have to make sacrifices which other branches of business do not have to share.

It should be observed that the relation between the quantity of bank notes and that of deposit money will not be the same in various countries. As I said before, this relation depends upon the demand of the public and this in its turn depends on the custom ary use of the various types of money in the country concerned. I hope that some of you will be interested in this subject and want to make a study of the relation of bank notes to deposit money in your own country and try to see whether any conclusions can be drawn from it as well as from possible changes in this relation.

The relatively steady relation between the circulation of bank notes and the quantity of deposit money is of great importance for the way in which monetary equilibrium should be achieved and maintained. Certainly not less important is a deviation from the normal relation between the two kinds of money. Such a deviation is a feature that should not be disregarded. On the contrary, if such deviations occur, we must try to find the cause and then endeavour to reach a satisfactory solution.

I must apologize for the fact that this introduction has been rather theoretical, but I believe that theoretical considerations can be of importance for modern banking.

I hope and trust that in the course of the Banking Summer School you will hear many interesting lectures and that the discussions will be held in an amicable and efficient way. I am also sure that the excursions will prove to be instructive and I sincerely hope that all of you will enjoy your stay in the Netherlands. I declare the 13th International Summer School to be open.

General Introduction to Medium Term Credit

BY C. A. KLAASSE

Managing Director Amsterdamsche Bank

When accepting the invitation to devote observations of a general and introductory nature to a subject one undertakes a somewhat ungrateful task. It means that the lecturer must throw light on the principal aspects of the subject without being able to deal exhaustively with any of them. It is therefore unavoidable that the speaker should fall into an incomplete and on many points unqualified argument, making the impression of giving a shallow and inadequate analysis of the subject. In doing so, the speaker benefits from one privilege, however: for the very reason that one cannot do more than make brief reference to the different problems to which the subject gives rise without too many reservations and qualifications, one may indulge in overstatements and understatements, which have the advantage of stimulating the exchange of views.

I should like my address to be understood in the light of these few words of introduction.

The institution of "credit" is a centuries-old concept, almost as old as the institution of "commerce" and as that of "medium of exchange," that is to say money. Credit is known in a virtually endless variety of forms, such as: suppliers' credit, buyers' credit, bank-advances, mortgages, debenture loans, treasury bills, etcetera. The purpose of the advance could vary to a great extent. Many centuries ago already loans were contracted to provide for the mercenaries' pay. And on into our times wars have caused the national debt to increase. Also, in the Middle Ages and even earlier, princes raised money on credit in order to build sumptuous palaces. Consumers' credit has been known in all centuries and has been greatly democratized in the last decades. All the same, the most important use of credit was and is of the commercial type, the financing of commerce and industry. It is to this kind of credit that I shall confine myself in this address.

For a long time already a distinction has been made between short-term credit and long-term credit. The former was regarded as credit serving for the financing of revolving working capital, the latter as credit for the financing of investments.

Short-term credit was generally assumed to be credit for the financing of transactions whose normal and natural settlement provided on short term the means to be applied towards redemption of the loan. If a term had to be mentioned, the period which parties had in mind did certainly not exceed the space of one year.

Long-term credit was considered, so far as credits to trade and industry were concerned, to be intended for the financing of objects not acquired in order to be sold again, but in order to be used, and in such a way that in the course of a certain number of years the sums set apart for depreciation would make the means available that could serve for redemption of the credit. Here again, therefore, there was question of a certain "self-liquidating" character, but spread over several years.

These school-examples of short-term and long-term credit still occur. Short-term, for instance, in the case of the financing of stocks of primary commodities, either sailing or stored, with traders. Long-term when a loan is specially contracted for the purchase of a certain investment object, say a ship that is let under bareboatcharter.

There is, however, nowadays an increasing number of credit transactions, both short-term and long-term, where any apparent link with specifically financed objects, either assets being part of a firm's working-capital or investments, hardly exists anymore. The position is rather such that there is a complex of loans as against a complex of objects financed through these credits. As regards the assets constituting the working-capital, that is to say stocks and accounts receivable, there is – seasonal and cyclical fluctuations excepted – as a rule a certain iron level which, though forever changing in its components, is constant in its collectivity. If such assets are financed by means of short-term credit it should be realized that such financing, though formally still quite in accordance with the above-mentioned design of self-liquidation, is no longer so materially, anyway not without interruption of the continuity. Such permanent components of the revolving assets therefore are likely to be financed rather by means of long-term capital, if this fits in with the financing structure of the business. Stocks of commodities thus may be financed by means of share capital, accounts receivable, preferably, by means of loan capital.

Also in the matter of investments there is a tendency for the financing being directed towards a collectivity rather than towards any specific asset. As a result of the uninterrupted expansion of most businesses there exists a certain continuity in investments, leading to capital being attracted on terms longer than the exact redemption period of the investment objects acquired with the credit.

The result of this development is that when long-term credit is taken up for the financing of part of the revolving working assets or of investments, the duration and conditions of redemption are often not only based on the pace at which funds become available again out of the objects procured with the credit but also on the usage prevailing or desired in the market. This usage which is itself again the historical result of the characteristics of demand and supply may differ according to the trend of interest rates.

On the basis of all this one may find short-term credit that is applied towards the financing of assets which either individually or seen as a collectivity require long-term capital, and long-term credit for the financing of assets which, if taken individually, would require short-term facilities. Side by side with this development one still notices the traditional use of short-term credits for the financing of essentially short-term requirements and long-term credit covering typically long-term financing needs.

The choice between short-term and long-term credit is sometimes made on purpose by the debtor in connection with the period for which he requires or thinks he will require the facility. In other cases, however, the choice depends on the possibilities he has. The standards parties granting long-term credit adopt for their judgements are often different from those used by the suppliers of short-term credit. For that reason the party demanding credit, whose requirements may very well tend towards attracting long-term funds, will sometimes find himself forced to put up with short credit, although it does not entirely conform to the structure of his financing.

This leads us to the question whether, and if so why, the markets for short-term and long-term credit are different. Why should lenders of funds on different terms differ? Why is not credit simply credit and has the period for which the credit is granted influence on the composition of the lending parties in the market? In the case of borrowers it is logical for the reasons stated before that there is a preference for short-term (repayable) or long-term credit.

Why does the supplier of credit too show a preference as to the duration of the advance?

Let us in this connection first consider the group of the commercial banks, which form one of the most important sources of short-term lending to industry and trade. The financing structure that is typical for the commercial bank is well-known: a relatively small capital of its own and an in comparison very large amount of funds entrusted to the bank by third parties. The period for which these funds have been placed at the disposal of the banks is never a long one. The proportion between demand deposits and time deposits differs from country to country. In the United States the emphasis has been rather on demand deposits, whereas in Europe rather on time deposits. Here too significant differences can be observed between various countries. In recent years there is e.g. a pronounced tendency in the Netherlands towards a shifting from demand to time. For the bulk of time deposits, however, a maximum period of one year exists. Putting aside the funds, which in some countries have been entrusted to the banks against "bons de caisse" with a life of 3 to 5 years and which compared with total bank resources are not very significant, one can state that the funds banks operate with, are of a typically short nature.

What are the considerations that make depositors "tie" their funds only for a short time? Leaving apart for the time being the money entrusted to the banks on savings-account – to which I shall return later on – one can maintain that the funds administered by the banks have in the eyes of their owners the character of liquid resources, either liquidities of first or of second order. The demand deposits are from the depositor's private standpoint primary liquid resources, and have from the point of vue of the community the character of money. Since the use of deposit money has more and more superseded the use of notes and coins, the banks have come to control in a forever growing degree the reservoir of deposit money. The money character of these balances implies inevitably that they must be callable at sight. Along with the primary liquid resources with money character the secondary liquid resources are entrusted to the banks. Within the circle of a year various expenditures give rise to a peak in the need for funds. As a rule in Europe dividends are paid only once a year, at most twice a year. Tax payment is another cause of peak requirements. Seasonal fluctuations, whether in connection with the harvestcycle or not, constitute still another ground for an undulating movement in the demand for liquid resources and finally mention must be made of the business cycle as a possible unforeseeable source for the need of liquid funds. All these factors cause industry to maintain liquid resources that need neither be immediately callable nor have the character of money although industry does require them to be at its disposal within a year's time.

These liquid resources can find employment for the time of their availability, either in the open money market or with the commercial banks. In each country the situation differs as regards the comparitive importance of the money market. In some countries there is hardly question or no question whatsoever of an open money market. On the other hand there are countries where the money market is an important instrument in the routing of industry's liquid resources.

Inasfar as these liquid resources are entrusted to the banks one can consider the commercial banks for that reason as a channel. Through this channel the funds, which the banks' customers have available, must find employment. It seems logical therefore to consider the banks as the typical suppliers of short-term credit. Even if one fully agrees with the thesis "loans create deposits" it does not make any difference, because this rule applies indeed exclusively to the banks as a collectivity. The individual bank can base its policy on the principle only that the source of its creditgiving power is formed by the deposits it attracts.

In just the same way as some funds in accordance with their destination are only available for short-term lending, other funds can be employed for a long period. Here one enters the field of savings, either saving for a distinct purpose or capital formation in general. Until and on into the beginning of this century these long-term resources originated mainly in the private sphere, that is the domain of private savers. In the last decade a drastic change has occurred in the composition of the supply of savings for long-term credit. The individual saver forms no longer the main opening for the flotation of long-term loan issues. His place has been taken by the institutional investor. Insurance companies, pension funds and savings banks belong to this group which accounts for the bulk of supply of long-term credit. Whereas the banks – and in countries with a well-developed money-market also companies with substantial secondary liquid resources – are the main parties on the supply side of the short-term credit market (for a duration up to one year), the institutional investors constitute to an increasing extent the majority of the market personnel on the supply side for long-term credit (for a duration of 10 years or more).

For two reasons those in command of long-term funds prefer to invest them equally for a long period. On the one hand the interest rate tends to be higher the longer the credit runs. In the second place life insurance companies and pension funds base themselves on a specific interest rate when calculating their premiums and building up their mathematical reserves.

It goes without saying that these institutional investors will strive to secure the interest rate for a long time, when investing their resources, in order to eliminate the risk of an adverse movement of the rate of interest.

This disposition will be the stronger the more the prevailing rates of interest are considered to be comparatively high and the more the possibility of a fall in interest rates is deemed to be real.

Owing to the aforementioned considerations there is consequently every reason, both because of motives on the side of suppliers of funds and on the demand side, to make a distinction between long-term and short-term credit.

Is there also a reason to regard medium-term credit as a financing instrument by itself? Just as there are in athletics sprinters and Marathon racers, but in between the specialists of the medium distance, and as among swimmers there are those who swim the Channel, 100-metre specialists, but also cracks on the medium-distances, thus there might with respect to credit terms likewise be reasons to distinguish not only between the two extremes, short-term and long-term, but also to give a special place to the medium-term.

There are only reasons to do so if there are real motives for such a clear-cut distinction on the side of borrowers as well as on that of lenders. In this case alone the basis exists for the development of a special market for such credit. For no separate market with a character of its own can grow and flourish but on the basis of parties that are typical for that market and whose mutual needs and wishes of demand and supply are attuned to each other. Now do these rules apply to medium-term credit?

If either the traditional suppliers of short-term credit or those of long-term credit or both would be equally willing to supply medium-term loans on the same conditions as their own specific type of credits, there would be no fundamental basis for the development of a typical medium-term loan market, even if there were borrowers with a strict and clear preference for that type of loan.

The fact that in the professional literature of many countries medium-term credit has been the subject of a great number of investigations and considerations might be looked upon as an indirect proof of the existence of a separate market, anyway of the need for a separate market for this description of credit.

Let us try in the first place to give an analysis of the motives on the part of borrowers which tend in the direction of medium credit terms. With reference to the above general considerations we would start from the assumption that such motives can only be based on the need of financing definite individual objects, and not on the financing of a collectivity of objects, because in that case there is always a certain continuity of the financing needs. That is why in this context we should think mainly of objects the acquisition of which bears a rather incidental and individual character, so that parties concerned do not foresee continuity with any degree of probability and therefore wish to adjust the financing incidentally to the duration of the need.

One of the classic examples which a few decades ago, in the United States, gave rise for the first time to a large-scale demand for medium-term credit was: the financing of oilrights, the purchase price of which, together with interest, could be amortized in a period of roughly 5 to 7 years. The growth of the market for these oilrights went along with the formation of a market for credit covering the period within which the financed project reproduced itself out of the yield and could therefore be amortized.

Another example is provided by the financing of aircraft. Before the jet airliners made their appearance, the period for writing off aircraft with piston engines varied from 5 to 7 years. In view of the rapid evolution of aero-engineering the air-line companies had to reckon with an economic life of their aircraft which was much shorter than the technical life. For the same reason it was extremely difficult to find a basis of financing suited to a continuous development, because the continuity was interrupted by abrupt innovations. It seemed exceedingly difficult to look far ahead into the future and to plan the financing. In many cases, therefore, fleet replacements were financed each time incidentally, anyway to a certain extent.

Beside aircraft there are many other means of production of which it can be said that the period within which such capital goods have earned their depreciation lies in the medium-term sphere. To a far greater extent than was the case a few decades ago, attention must be paid to the fact that the technological advance leads up to the situation that long before the end of its technical life an investment cannot compete anymore, economically, with modern apparatus, which either can be worked with less labour, or gives a considerably greater production per unit, or turns out a better quality. The comparatively strong rise in the cost of labour during the past few decades has promoted this phenomenon, or at least accentuated it.

The estimated economic life of investments differs, from case to case, much more than does the technical life, and acquisitions, moreover, are ordered much more irregularly than in the past. Formerly a business that had been built up gradually through continuous extension and worked with traditional apparatus, which was not subject to sudden revolutionary changes due to new inventions, could have a more or less flowing structure of financing, in which depreciation and replacements were virtually in a state of equilibrium.

Nowadays the investment activity often proceeds with sudden jerks, and on that account business leaders are more often induced to finance incidental acquisitions in an incidental way, the redemption being adapted to the often relatively short pay-out time, with the result that the need of medium-term financing is felt more often than in bygone times.

In this connection mention should be made also of the greatly increased volume of financing by means of the instalment-payment system during the past few decades. This form of granting credit, which in the United States flourished already before the second World War, has shown a considerable expansion in Europe, too, especially in the post-war period. This applies to the financing of durable consumer goods as well as of specific production goods. As regards the latter category special mention may be made of trucks, motor buses, tractors and draglines. In all these cases the rule applies that the term of financing is adapted to the period in which the borrowing business can supply the redemption out of the amortization of the financed objects. In the case of the durable consumer goods the duration of the credit depends on the ability of the consumer to set aside part of his income for the redemption of the credit.

And finally I would mention as one of the typical sources for the demand of medium-term credit, which in recent years, in Europe, has been in the centre of interest: the granting of export credits. The need of capital goods in the under-developed areas, where domestic capital formation lags far behind the need, has had as a result that the buyers of such goods request suppliers for credits covering a large portion of the purchase price. One can say that the situation in this respect has developed in such a way that the granting of credit has become an important element in the competitive struggle, beside the factors of price and quality.

Of course the exporting industries cannot allow this kind of credit out of their own means, and consequently we have here again a source of demand for credit to cover these export financing facilities which, generally speaking, are allowed for medium terms.

Thus there are a multitude of phenomena that can be referred to as causing a growing demand for medium-term credit. On the side of the demand, therefore, we have adequately analysed the problem. As mentioned before, however, there must be motives on the side of the credit supply, too, creating preference for or an aversion against this specific credit term with lenders, if a separate market is to spring up and develop.

What are the aspects of the problem on the side of the supply? Both as regards short-term credit and long-term credit it can be said that the sources feeding the supply are different. And as the use and spending of the credits also create typical seekers for short-term as well as for long-term credit, the conditions for the formation of specific markets for those two forms are fulfilled.

How then is the situation as regards the supply of medium-term credit? Are there typical parties operating in this field who are prepared to offer medium-term credit only and neither long-term nor short-term credit in any case not on the same conditions? Or are there among the traditional suppliers of short-term or of long-term credit also a number who are interested in supplying medium-term credit as well, and if so is there any reason for reticence in this special field?

It is difficult to give an answer to this question without falling into quite a number of qualifications and reserves. The situation, in fact, differs considerably not only per country, but also in respect of time. Forms of financing are upon the whole strongly dependent on tradition. When the need for new forms, new conditions, arises, it usually takes some considerable time before the principles on which the tradition is based have been sufficiently reformed to be able to speak of the creation of a new tradition. Everything is flowing, also in the matter of financing tradition, but the evolution takes time, every now and then a long time.

What objections do the traditional suppliers of short-term credit and of long-term credit have against the medium-term? As mentioned before, the basic philosophy of the commercial banks, the typical suppliers of short-term credit, has been for years on end the following: out of funds entrusted on short term only credits can be granted which are repayable at short notice. The maintenance of liquidity, which beside solvency is the highest asset of banking, ranked uppermost on the list of desiderata of the business policy.

A few observations should be made in this connection. As long as the granting of credits by the commercial banks was limited to separate self-liquidating goods transactions one could say that the formal liquidity of the short-term credit rested also on material, that is to say natural, liquidity of the financed transaction.

However, when extending the granting of credits, to include

also the financing of stocks of goods and accounts receivable, the formal liquidity was maintained, it is true, by the possibility of withdrawing the overdraft-facility or through the technique of financing by bills of exchange, but viewed from the point of the collectivity of the banks on the one hand and the collectivity of the borrowers on the other hand this natural liquidity was more dream than reality.

Without disorganizing economic life completely no large-scale liquidation of bank-credits of this nature would be possible. Collectively it could at best be a question of "deduced liquidity", based that is on rediscount at or borrowing from the central bank.

As a matter of fact banks in several countries have for a long time already invested on medium-term an important part of the funds deposited with them at comparatively short notice; yet these banks were not afraid that this might jeopardize their liquidity. In the United Kingdom as well as in the United States and some Scandinavian countries banks, for many years, have possessed considerable holdings of government bonds with maturities that may be counted among the medium if not the long terms. Such an investment policy was not considered to be contrary to the principles of liquidity, because the government bonds that were held by the banks were readily marketable. The banks relied on the possibility of selling the bonds, if necessary, though they realized that this might entail rather substantial losses, as in fact often occurred. The disadvantages of this investment policy, consequently, were considered to lie in the sphere of the profitability rather than in that of the liquidity.

The situation is quite different, however, with respect to the medium-term credits granted to trade and industry for the aforementioned purposes. There is no possibility in this case of having recourse to an open market, anyway generally speaking not. Here again, however, there is sometimes another factor on which "deduced liquidity" can be based, namely in those countries where it is possible to rediscount bills with a medium-term life with the central bank, either directly or indirectly through a special rediscount institution. Especially in the field of export transactions that require medium term financing such facilities exist in some European countries.

For the said reasons the orthodox theory of banking policy in many countries rejected on principle and for a considerable time the medium-term credit to industry as being contrary to the fundamental rules of sound banking. During the last few decades, however, gradual and in some countries even abrupt changes have been noticeable in the approach.

In spite of the objections outlined before commercial banks in a growing number of countries can be found to show a tendency to enter the field of medium-term credit. It is remarkable that this tendency was first observable in the United States, where upon the whole the banking system was organized on the classic anglo-saxon lines of the deposit bank with the underlying philosophy: "Only short-term credit out of short-term funds". And it is perhaps even more remarkable that when in the thirties this evolution in the granting of credits initiated the term-loan, this was not in the first place the result of any urgent fresh need on the part of business life, to which the banks willy-nilly yielded. On the contrary, it was rather the banks themselves which, faced with the problem of superfluous liquidity, offered the medium-term credit to their industrial customers, thus competing with the traditional suppliers of long-term credit. Since the birth of the medium-term bank-credit the comparitive significance of this form of financing has passed various phases in the United States. There were periods in which the term-loan decreased in importance, and there were times when the urge for this financing came from the industry, especially in periods of a tight market for long-term credit and when interest rates in that market were relatively high. Industry in such periods had recourse to their bankers, not invariably to the joy and satisfaction of the latter. Particularly not when such a concentrated demand for term-loans coincided with a large general demand for short-term bank-credit, thus forcing the banks to liquidate part of their medium-term market investments at a loss.

However this may be, it can now be said that for a considerable time already there has been no question anymore in the United States of a fundamental dislike of medium-term credit on the part of the commercial banks.

In Europe the evolution in the ideas of the banks in the matter of medium-term credit lags somewhat behind the American notions, and certainly it cannot yet be said that the new form of credit has been generally adopted here. In the first place the problem, presented itself in an acute form in Europe much later, after the second World War, when in particular the medium-term export credit for the supply of capital goods brought the problem to a head. An exception must perhaps be made with respect to the evolution in France where as early as 1918 the need for medium-term credit was distinctly felt.[1] In most countries the banks at first stuck to the dogma: "only short-term credit out of short-term funds". When nevertheless they wished to enter the field of medium-term credits, either for the financing of instalment-payment transactions, export transactions, or for the financing of equipment in general, they often did so via subsidiary institutions. The latter, with or without the guarantee of the parent bank, provided for their own passive financing, which as regards term was adapted as much as possible to that of the loans granted.

In Europe, too, a clear tendency is now noticeable, however, to regard the medium-term credit as an admissible instrument also for use by the commercial banks themselves.

Several factors have contributed to the fact that the liquidity of the banks is now regarded in a light different from that prevailing some decades ago. In the first place more recent experience has shown that a great measure of stability is noticeable in the collectivity of customers' funds entrusted to the banks. Stability is even rather an understatement in this connection. The fact is that in almost all countries deposits with the banks have constantly risen, mainly unfortunately, as a result of the practically uninterrupted inflationary developments. Whereas up to the thirties financial crises occurred to the accompaniment of economic depressions, during the past thirty years financial crises and the accompanying runs on the banks have not happened anymore. For that matter really serious depressions have not been in evidence

[1] The main reason was the enormous upsurge of credit demand as a result of the general wish to make up for the gap in investments, which had arisen during the war, when normal replacements had inevitably been postponed. With savings for the same reason at a low level the supply of long-term credit was quite insufficient to meet the demand. A manifest tendency developed to employ the funds concentrated with the banks who, still sticking to the liquidity rule, were yet not willing to grant long-term loans. In order to be of assistance, however, they founded subsidiaries, which were to provide the necessary means. All the same, the importance of these institutions at the time should not be exaggerated.

either during this period and one gets more and more the impression that the multifarious measures for the control of cyclical developments – whether they are deliberately intended to do so or not – have indeed the effect of making the economic ups and downs far less striking.

It cannot be denied that in this connection, too, the situation differs per country. In a small country, where the economy depends greatly on international trade, comparatively important shifts in the balance of payments relations may occur, which at once have their repercussion on the domestic liquidity picture. Even if corrective measures are taken against such a development, the effect of such measures is subject to a certain timelag. In countries of the kind, among which the Netherlands must doubtless be reckoned, the banks consequently should count less on stability of the volume of funds deposited with them. Therefore they should follow a relatively more conservative and cautious liquidity policy. The same remark applies to countries which are typical ports of refuge for internationally migrating capitals.

A second factor to be mentioned in this connection is the generally increasing significance of the share of the commercial banks in the administration of the country's savings. It is a more or less generally accepted thesis that monies on savings accounts, viewed as a collectivity, have a functional significance that differs, both economically and monetarily, from that of the creditor balances and time deposits entrusted to the commercial banks. Whereas the latter two groups of funds are part of the total domestic liquid resources whilst the creditor balances moreover belong to the quantity of money in circulation, this is not the case with savings. It is generally considered correct to regard savings balances as funds intended for the capital market, which can be invested on long term.

Two plainly demonstrable factors, therefore, which might justify the banks' altered attitude with respect to medium-term credit. In this connection it should also be remembered that when a portfolio of medium-term investments is gradually built up the possibility exists of obtaining a well-balanced holding, evenly spread out over various maturity dates, from which a relatively important amortization quota is regularly becoming available. Even if one reckons with deflationary developments and declining general liquidity, one may, as long as no calamities happen, consider the liquidity of the bank assured because of the natural "expiration" of the portfolio.

We have up to now discussed the banks as possible sources for medium-term credits, that is to say as potential parties on the supply side of the market for such credits. In view of the fact that the medium term by its own nature is situated between the short and the long term it seems logical to pay attention also to the attitude which the traditional suppliers of long-term credit take up with respect to the medium-term credit. In contrast with the banks, considerations of liquidity can play a lesser part here. Again the situation differs from country to country. In several countries it has been customary for years on end to issue bonds and debentures with diverging maturities, varying from short 2-year notes to perpetual loans. In such countries the medium-term credit is hardly a special problem. In many other countries, however, the capital market is used only to the issue of long-term loans, 15-years or more. The increasing significance of the group of institutional investors, such as life assurance companies, pension-funds etc. as suppliers of capital has the tendency to prolong the term of bonds and debentures, since these institutions acquire investments to cover their long-running obligations. Especially when the market rates of interest are satisfactory in comparison with the "calculatory" rate of interest underlying the mathematical reserves, there will be a tendency to make the life of the investments as long as possible.

This goes to explain why in the initial period of the demand for medium-term credit on a growing scale it was difficult to interest parties belonging to this group in this type of investment. This was true even in countries where, as in Holland, the institutional investors, especially the insurance companies, used to act on a large scale as lenders in the mortgage market, for which the duration is generally fixed at five years. Incidentally it may be observed that this form of credit is surely the most unorthodox one can imagine as here, clearly, long-term investments are financed by means of medium-term credit, while on the other hand the short duration of the loan often does not fit at all in the financing structure of the lending institution.

However, in this field too an evolution is on its way in several countries. Particularly in cases where cooperation is possible between commercial banks and institutional investors in such a manner that the relatively shorter running parts, up to say 4 or 5 years, are furnished by the banks and the longer running peak of the credit by the institutional investors, the latter can more easily pass over the threshold of their resistance against medium-term credit.

Now in overlooking the situation on the supply side of the medium-term credit we can say that in the period of take-off run of the demand for this type of loans there existed undoubtedly a gap, as both the traditional suppliers of short- term credit and those of long-term credit were hesitant to meet this demand. As is often the case with fresh developments in the economic field, here too a gradual evolution has taken place with both categories of lenders, to such an extent that there is now virtually no question any longer of a gap in this market. However, this means at the same time that one can hardly speak of a market with a character of its own for the medium-term credit, because the condition of the existence of a group of parties typical for the supply side of the market has not been fulfilled. The borrowers on this term can by and large be served in one of the two traditional markets or in both, perhaps in combination with each other, namely the markets for long-term and short-term credit.

This does not mean that in certain circumstances or in certain countries it might not be difficult to find a sufficient supply of medium-term credit. In periods in which a decline of the rate of interest in the capital market is expected, the willingness among potentially long-term investors, viz. assurance companies and pension funds, to grant medium-term credits will diminish. Yet it should also be remembered that in quite a number of countries it is usual for borrowers, also in the case of long-term loans, to reserve the possibility of anticipated redemption after a certain period. The shorter term of the credit therefore will often not be quite prohibitive if compensation is given by means of an adequate offer of interest.

As regards the banks as sources for medium-term credit it should be realized that although the resistance founded on old principles against the granting of medium-term credit has decreased perceptibly all along the line, and although one gets the impression that the evolution of the philosophy underlying their business-policy is rapidly making headway, yet the liquidity notion will put a certain limit to the granting of these credits. Especially in periods of great demand for short-term commercial loans the willingness to grant medium-term credit is apt to decline. Of great influence in this connection is also the policy of the central bank in the matter of credit control. This is true in particular in countries where the banks depend more or less permanently on the financing-support of the central bank. If the banks must regularly rediscount part of their bill portfolio with the central bank, the possibility of granting medium-term credits will depend largely on the rediscount regulations.

In this connection it seems adequate to devote yet a few words to the monetary aspect of the medium-term credit, though it will be clear that this can only be done very briefly and, consequently, incompletely in the framework of this general address.

Does the medium-term credit present any specific monetary aspects?

If and insofar as this kind of credit is supplied by institutional investors, which obtain their means from collective savings, there is no question of any difference in monetary effect with the normal granting of long-term credit by these institutions. Credit supplied out of current savings is, no matter in what form and for what term it is given, deemed to be monetary neutral. Now if the funds for medium-term credits are obtained from the reservoir of the resources of the commercial banks, is there any reason then to suspect that the monetary effect will differ from that of the granting of short-term business loans by the banks to trade and industry? If we assume as working-hypothesis that medium-term credit is always used for investment purposes and short-term business credit for the financing of inventories, including unfinished products, and of accounts receivable, is there any reason in that to pass different judgement on the two kinds of credit as to the monetary effect? In its generality this question can certainly not be answered in the affirmative. In both cases the credits procure purchasing power for the borrower either for raw materials, semi-manufactured goods, finished products, or capital goods. In both cases the granting of the loans may have an inflationary effect, but in neither of the two cases does this effect make itself felt in all circumstances. It can be said, though, that in the case of short-term credits the possibility of applying corrections to any undesirable monetary development by means of credit-restricting measures, is more apparent. It is possible, if the economic consequences of such a measure are accepted, to force down the volume of short-term credit. In the case of medium-term credits this is naturally not possible at short notice, although if the portfolio is evenly spread over various maturities it may to a certain extent be achieved too.

Summing up then I would conclude that taking into account the evolution of ideas in the matter of business policy of banks and institutional investors during recent years, it can hardly be said in most countries that the medium-term credit still constitutes a real problem. This is true from the individual lender's standpoint and, to an important extent, holds also good in the general economic, that is the monetary, sphere.

I think that I have fulfilled my task to give you a bird's-eye view of the most important aspects of the problem of medium-term credit and their historical development in the framework of a changing world and consequently changing attitudes as regards certain principles of business-policy. As I said in the beginning the speaker in charge of a general introduction to the problem may indulge to a certain extent in over- and understatements. I may have made use of this privilege. But it has to be borne in mind that sometimes developments take place with such speed that what is an overstatement to-day may be a well-established principle to-morrow.

The Amsterdam Stock Exchange and Its Function in Government and Corporate Financing

By P. F. J. de Kok
Chairman of the Amsterdam Stock Exchange

I am very happy to have the opportunity to give to you by way of an introduction to your visit to our Exchange an address on some aspects of the Amsterdam Stock Exchange and its function in government and corporate financing.

The history of this Exchange is so full of interesting events, that I would be able to talk to you about it for a long time. Instead, however, I prefer to draw some brief outlines, along which I will give you a general view of the significance of this stock exchange for Holland in the past and in recent times.

As main points of this address I have chosen first of all some historical aspects and the part the Amsterdam Stock Exchange played in the past.

After that I shall deal with some aspects of corporate financing in this country and of the part played by the Exchange in connection with the conversion of privately owned companies into public corporations.

How the Stock Exchange works will be the next subject of this speech, after which I will discuss some recent trends in the field of investment and security analysis and finally I would like to tell you, how I see the near future of this Exchange.

I now will begin by telling you something about the history of the Amsterdam Stock Exchange which goes back to the beginning of the 17th century. In those days – in 1602 to be exact – the foundation took place of the Dutch East India Company, a shipping undertaking which acquired from the Dutch Government the monopoly of the trade to the East Indies.

The company's structure was of the character of what might be called to-day a limited liability company and in the world of those days it was something quite new, also by the size of its capital – six million Guilders – and the way in which it raised money by issuing shares for subscription by the public.

In Amsterdam which was a leading financial centre, there was an active trade in those shares on the corners of the streets or, on rainy days, under the porches of shops. As the favourable results of the company's activities strongly appealed to public imagination, there soon appeared a lot of speculative buying and selling of the shares, not only by Dutchmen but also by foreigners. For instance, the French Ambassador to the Dutch Republic held so considerable an interest in the Dutch East India Company that he successfully blocked plans in his own country to establish a competing French East India Company.

As soon as bearer bonds had made their appearance it became obvious that the Exchange could also perform a significant function in the field of public loans. This took place at about the middle of the 17th century and these securities came likewise to be traded by the stockbrokers.

He who, in the 17th century, could not afford to buy shares in the Dutch East India Company, could invest his money also in municipal or government loans. For the more wealthy people there were moreover the loans issued by the Boards of the big "polder" works. The shares of the East India Company were at first mostly traded in parcels of 20 shares, so-called "regimenten," which involved an amount of about 300.000 Guilders.

Soon also foreign securities enjoyed the interest of Dutch investors. As far as we know the first foreign loan granted by Amsterdam bankers was the one given to the Elector of Brandenburg in 1616, to be followed by many loans to other European princes.

In the 17th and 18th centuries money often was so cheap in the Low Countries, that the rate of interest here was substantially lower than, for instance, in England and France. It is known that in the 18th century England financed its numerous wars on the Continent partly by means of loans issued on the Amsterdam capital market. In this respect it is significant to mention that in 1777 59 million Pounds of the English public debt, that is about 42%, was owned by Dutch investors.

That this country could play such an important part in the field of government financing was largely due to the existence of a well-organized stock market which made it possible to place the loans with a large group of investors.

The Napoleonic times marked the end of this first period of prosperity.

Not until the second half of the 19th century did the international capital market of Amsterdam revive.

After 1860 the Amsterdam stock market grew rapidly in importance when the Amsterdam bankers succeeded in securing a strong position in financing many quickly expanding American corporations, such as the railway companies in the Southern part of the United States.

Although a large, sometimes even controlling, interest was held in railway companies like Southern Railways and Kansas City Southern, Dutch financial interests did not confine themselves to the Southern states only. Capital requirements were enormous in the whole of the United States, which was partly a result of the opening up of the West and partly due to the losses suffered in the Civil War.

The financing of American railways by The Netherlands reached a peak in 1871 when in the time of one year as much as 72 million Dollars of new bonds were introduced at the Amsterdam Stock Exchange.

The number of foreign securities listed in Amsterdam increased sharply in the years 1865 – 1875.

In 1865 the number of foreign stocks listed was 89 – mainly government loans – but ten years later it had grown to 188, including stocks and bonds of no less than 91 railway companies. As the American economic position became stronger and stronger, the Dutch interest gradually increased also. Besides the stocks of railway companies, also mining, industrial and public utility shares were listed on the Amsterdam market, and in the end there was practically no American corporation of some importance whose shares were not officially listed here.

This explains why until World War II the Amsterdan Stock Exchange was the biggest market for American securities outside the United States. Even to-day the shares of over 200 American corporations are listed in Amsterdam. Moreover the Stock List publishes the prices of quite a number of American bonds. The volume of trading in these American securities has however diminished quite considerably since the war.

The Dutch Dollar interests, which were 600 to 800 million

Dollars in 1914, had by August 1939 increased to 1,8 billion Dollars.

Although after 1850 the Dutch clearly showed a preference to invest in American securities, up till World War I, Russian and Austrian government loans also were much in favour here. Also Brazilian and other Latin-American stocks had a large market in Amsterdam.

Besides these foreign investments the Amsterdam Stock Exchange gave a very considerable support to the financing of sugar, tobacco and rubber estates and the development of mineral wealth in the former Netherlands East Indies, now Indonesia.

To illustrate this I can tell you that in 1914 Dutch investments in foreign countries were estimated at over three billion Guilders and those in Indonesia at about one billion Guilders. Before the last war the Estates section of the Amsterdam Stock Exchange was one of the busiest and liveliest of the market. An important part of our national wealth consisted of the revenues of these investments in the former Netherlands East Indies and through the Amsterdam Stock Exchange substantial amounts were invested in shipping, trade and industry in that area.

The turn of events in South-East Asia has of course effected these shares in their importance for the Amsterdam market.

If in the past Dutch investors showed a marked preference for investments outside their country, in the course of the current century this tendency gradually has changed, and as a consequence this has also altered the character of the Amsterdam Stock Exchange. More and more attention was given to investment opportunities in The Netherlands itself.

As a matter of fact the growth of the manufacturing industries in The Netherlands and, as a consequence thereof the increasing demand for capital, led to a tightening of the ties between banking and industry, and between industry and the Amsterdam Stock Exchange. A great many corporations had to find the means for their expansion by opening up external resources and by issuing shares through the Amsterdam Stock Exchange. Once the road to the stock market had been opened the financial implications of the expansion appeared to offer considerably less difficulty than before.

Apparently Dutch investors at first had to conquer some hesitation before they were willing to entrust their money to local industries and so the corporate financing was at first often arranged by issuing preferred shares, as these were likely to make people feel that they had chosen a safer investment than in common stock with uncertain dividends.

By issuing new stock and by placing them with the investors through the intermediary of the Amsterdam Stock Exchange some Dutch companies succeeded to accelerate their rate of expansion and to grow into huge organizations with world-wide interests. In this connection I would mention Royal Dutch which at the moment is the biggest industrial company in the world outside the United States, Philips' Lamps, Unilever and A.K.U.

The successful post-war expansion of the Dutch economy began to draw the attention of foreign investors to the investment merits of the shares of the bigger Dutch companies. And in the last few years considerable amounts of Dutch securities were bought by foreign investors. Before the second world war blocks of Dutch shares were already held abroad, but their value was only a fraction of the considerable amounts invested by foreigners in Dutch shares after this war, and especially after June 1954, when the shares of Royal Dutch were officially listed on the New York Stock Exchange. At first such purchases mainly consisted of shares of this company, but soon foreign investors began to discover the merits of Philips' Lamps, Unilever and finally also of Hoogovens (Royal Dutch Blast Furnaces) and some of the smaller companies. A.K.U. became popular in Germany.

In the last 5 or 6 years nearly four billion Guilders worth of Dutch securities have been sold abroad. As far as we know the buyers were mainly American, German, Swiss, Belgian and French private investors and investment companies.

As a result of these purchases the Dutch holdings of the leading stocks on the Amsterdam Stock Exchange were reduced considerably. According to information released some time ago Dutch investors were holding only about 27% of the outstanding shares of Royal Dutch, 45% of the shares of Philips' Lamps and 55% of the shares of Unilever N.V.. As these securities are in the hands of many investors in Europe and the United States and are listed on various exchanges, they have typically assumed the character of international securities. This means that in the last few years these leading Dutch securities have become the features of the international arbitrage trade, which trade rather is a speciality of the Dutch bankers and brokers.

I now would like to tell you something more about the role the Amsterdam Stock Exchange played in the financing of the industrialization of the Netherlands and also about the consequences of the concentration in industry and banking for our Stock Exchange.

It was not before the last decades of the nineteenth century that the Amsterdam Stock Exchange began to play an important part in the financing of local industry. Until then, the private banks, which did most of the issuing business, had mainly been engaged in issuing national and foreign loans. Industrial corporations in this country were still relatively small at that time, and quite often they were family owned companies that could be financed from internally generated funds.

With the acceleration of the industrial expansion, internal financing reached its limits and the need for outside financing became more urgent. It was in this respect that the Amsterdam Stock Exchange could offer its services as an intermediary between the investors and the companies that needed new capital. It should be noted however that businessmen in this country continued to have a strong preference for internal financing.

The industrial expansion I just mentioned has been one of the factors that led to the concentration in the Dutch banking system. Small independent banks often were unable to bear the risks involved in granting credits to the constantly expanding industry.

This led to many mergers in the banking business and to the formation of some big branch banks which have their head offices in Amsterdam and Rotterdam. From these centres they can exert a considerable control on the granting of credits to companies all over the country. The great number of branch offices and an efficient management made a better spread of the risks possible. This development has been favourable to the industrialization of the Netherlands because credits, both in the commercial and industrial field, could be increased substantially.

If concentration favoured the economic expansion by bigger

credits, it should be observed that on the other hand the commercial banks could – through current account and anticipatory credits – exert an increasing influence on the methods of financing applied by company managers. This has opened the way for the big commercial banks to enter the issuing or underwriting business.

Until the beginning of this century private bankers were most active in the underwriting business in this country, whereas the activities of the big banks in this field were only moderate. This however has changed gradually and at present an important part of the issuing business for local stocks has passed into the hands of the big banks.

In this country independent issuing houses or underwriting firms do not exist.

Concentration has not been confined to industry and to the banking system alone. Similar tendencies can after 1945 be recognized in the national supply and demand of capital. On the supply side an increasing amount of national savings are concentrated with the institutional investors. In recent years the latter managed greatly to strenghten their influence on the capital market. There is also a concentration of the demand for long term capital. On the one hand this results from company mergers, while on the other hand it is brought about by the government's policy of practically concentrating the demand for long term capital of provincial and municipal governments with one central institution, the so-called "Bank for Netherlands Municipalities."

The concentration tendencies have, of course, furthered a direct contact between those who supply long term capital and those who need it. This means that, in assessing the function of the Amsterdam Stock Exchange and the possibilities of its development, one should take into account that:

(1) the method of financing from internally generated funds will continue to be important for many companies;

(2) direct contacts between the suppliers of capital and those who need it, will continue to compete with financing through the intermediary of the Stock Exchange.

With regard to the first point I however have to mention that in the Bill and Corporation Tax 1960, recently presented to Parliament, the Netherlands Minister of Finance has suggested alteration of the uniform scale into a differentiated scale, by which the rate of taxation of the company of paid-out profits will be 15 points below the rate applicable to retained profits.

I now ask your attention for some of the more technical aspects of the securities business in this country. In this respect I want to tell you first of all something about the listing of securities on this stock exchange.

Contrary to those countries, where the admission of a security to the official quotation has been made dependent on the consent of public or semi-public organizations, the listing of a security on the Amsterdam Stock Exchange is a question that is in the first place dealt with by the Committee of the Stock Exchange. True, there is a Stock Exchange Act (dating from 1914) which provides that the ultimate consent depends on a decision of the Minister of Finance, but the technical supervision and the drawing up of the listing rules are in fact entirely left to the Amsterdam Stock Exchange. An institution like for instance the Securities and Exchange Commission in the United States does not exist here.

The rules that are of primary importance in connection with an application for official listing have been laid down in the so-called "Fondsenreglement" (Rules on listing securities).

One of the most important documents published in case of new issues or introduction is, as we all know, the prospectus. It is clear that on this point the Rules go into great detail and contain a long list of conditions which a prospectus should satisfy. It is particularly in the matter of the prospectus that requirements have been made more and more servere in recent years.

Before a prospectus is published, a thorough consultation takes place as a rule between the bank that acts as issuing agent and the officials of the Amsterdam Stock Exchange. Apart from this, many discussions have in the meantime been held between the bank and the company with a view to collecting the data necessary to satisfy the requirements of the Stock Exchange.

Also the need is felt of further improvement of company publications and of greater publicity regarding companies which wish to raise or have raised already capital by way of a public issue.

To stimulate company managements to improve their Annual Reports a number of "Oscars" are awarded in this country. It is gratifying to find that many good results have for some years been recorded in this respect and that the quality of reports to shareholders is improving gradually.

One further aspect of the activities of the members of the Stock Exchange that may interest you refers to the issue of certificates of shares by administration offices. These certificates may be compared to American Depositary Receipts (A.D.R.'s) which are so well known in the United States. "Certificate" and "Administration Office" are not new terms. They date as far back as the early nineteenth century, when administration offices created bearer certificates for registered government bonds, in order to meet the marked preference of the Dutch investors for bearer securities.

The administration office certificate also appeared to be useful in stimulating the investment in American securities, which in this respect operates as follows. One buys American shares in New York against which bearer certificates in Holland are issued. Dividends and other distributions, which are paid by check to the administration office as holder of the original registered shares, are passed on to the certificate holders (after deduction of a certain fee) against surrender of one of the coupons attached to the certificates. On account of the small denominations of the American stocks the Dutch certificates are mainly issued in units of 5 or 10 shares.

Besides the certificates for foreign stocks, the official list includes also certificates for domestic securities. These are, as a rule, issued by administration offices for the purpose of bringing security holdings within the reach of the small investor. This is done by making a number of small denominations available to represent the original securities.

I now turn to the actual trade on the Stock Exchange. The rules that are of importance in this respect are primarily the "Rules for the trade in securities", which contain regulations concerning the purchase and sale of securities and their delivery, and concerning the various kinds of dealings, such as for instance cash dealings and optional dealings.

The "Rules on Quotation" regulate the price determination, the requirements quotations have to satisfy in order to be inserted in the official price list, the way of reporting prices made, and the way of reporting the volume of securities traded.

As regards the organization and the mechanism of the trade I would observe the following.

On the floor of the Amsterdam Stock Exchange some 600 to 700 persons – members and their authorized and unauthorized clerks – meet every day except Saturdays, Sundays and holidays. Part of them come to execute orders for clients (stock brokers), others are specialists in a number of listed stocks. The latter are called "hoeklieden" and it should be noted that their function is somewhat different from that of the specialists on the New York Stock Exchange. There are also members doing business for their own account (professional dealers), and furthermore arbitrageurs and floor brokers.

The floor is divided into 82 spaces and a certain number of stocks designated by the Committee on Quotations is traded in each space. In local market jargon the spaces are called "hoeken" or pitches and one may compare them with the "posts" on the New York Stock Exchange. In the "pitches" transactions are effected by what I called the specialists who act as middlemen between buyers and sellers. At the close of the market this specialist will determine the price of a stock on the basis of the orders received by him, in such a way, that a maximum number of orders can be executed. For this intermediary the specialist is paid a brokerage. The official Price List is drawn up under the supervision of the Commissioner on Quotations, a member of the Stock Exchange Committee.

Stocks which on account of certain qualities may be classed as so-called "active" stocks are often traded in so-called "open" pitches, where buyers and sellers are shouting out their bid or selling prices, which may lend great animation to the scene on the floor. For these stocks the marking of transactions takes place in seven periods or "tapes." The highest and lowest quotation of each tape are marked separately in the Price List.

The selling members must report to the Committee their total sales of each security. These figures are added together per security and are likewise marked in the Price List.

As the Amsterdam Stock Exchange hours (1.15 to 2.30 p.m.) are not the same as in other European financial centres and in view of the fact that an extensive international trade has gradually developed in securities quoted both in Amsterdam and elsewhere, the Amsterdam arbitrageurs felt the need to do business also at other hours of the day. To that end a group of floor brokers is present in the stock exchange building in the morning before the market opens and in the afternoon after the official hours.

In the past the clients of most members of the Amsterdam Stock Exchange were largely private investors but this has changed considerably in recent years as a result of the growing importance of institutional investors. The number and size of trust funds which have money available for investment in securities have greatly increased. Owing to this development the function of the members as investment advisers has also been subject to change. In the past investment recommendations to private investors were often mainly based on knowledge of the trade and on market experience. Gradually, however, people have come to attach greater value to the study of the long-range market outlook and to security analysis. As a result the current market price and the last-paid dividend have become less important factor in the determination of investment policies.

One of the consequences has been that bankers and banking institutions and also stock broking firms have for some years been employing an increasing number of people with the special duties of keeping a detailed economic documentation, drawing up memoranda on certain stocks and groups of stocks, analysing developments in certain industries, and preparing scrupulously composed market reports.

This trend in the field of investment advice and security analysis is symptomatic of the past decade and there are many indications that this process will be accelerated in the years ahead. The influence of American analysts is noticeable in this respect.

I have now come to the final part of my address.

Although no one is allowed to look into the future and to see what will happen in the months and years to come, I feel that there are some trends that will probably be extended in the future and which can serve as a guidance for the line of conduct we are now trying to determine.

For instance, one will surely have to reckon with a continued concentration of national savings in the hands of institutions. As social development is proceeding the urge for the creation of social security may be expected to increase rather than diminish. This will further the formation of trust and pension funds and as these funds have obligations that can be expressed in nominal amounts, the formation of these funds will cause a further concentration of non-risk bearing capital in the hands of a relatively small number of institutions. One may assume that these institutions will try to make a considerable part of their investments directly without the intermediary of the Stock Exchange.

This might be interpreted as a tendency unfavourable to the stock exchange. It should be observed, however, that, as in many other countries, an awareness is more and more widely felt that the post-war economic policy – which on the one hand aims at full employment and on the other hand at curbing inflation – arouses a conflicting situation which in the past had sometimes been decided in favour of full employment and not of monetary stability.

This has been a reason why we notice an increasing urge to invest a greater part of the trust funds in shares than was done in the pre-war period. This trend may at least for some time continue to have a beneficial effect on the stock exchange.

A second line which may be extended in the years before us is the concentration tendency in banking. This, we may assume, has not yet come to an end. As a result the branch bank system will find scope for further development. As the branch banks are members of the Amsterdam Stock Exchange, this development creates the possibility – according as the number of branches increases and the distance between any house and a branch office declines – of bringing the stock market closer to the private investor.

So the growth of the branch banks may result in a broadening of the stock trade and a greater spread of information on the stock market and the securities traded. This may also be beneficial to the Amsterdam Stock Exchange.

As the next line likely to be extended into the future I would point to the development of the European economic integration and particularly the co-operation within the European Economic Community.

This integration is in the first place developing in the field of goods and services, the visible items in the balance of payments. One may assume, however, that integration will not stop there and that capital movements will be liberated in a following stage.

This will mean that the capital markets within the Common Market area will be drawn closer together and that the stock markets will also come to closer co-operation. During discussions among the committees of the Western-European bourses it appeared that contacts more intensive than before are deemed most useful.

How this integration process will come off, nobody can say. In any case a closer co-operation will only be practicable if there is a mutual preparedness to make certain sacrifices and if consideration is given to the extent to which specialization of activities will be possible.

In this integration process the Amsterdam Stock Exchange may make an important contribution. This Exchange has through the centuries held the reputation of a decidedly international market. It must be possible, I believe, for it to maintain and even strengthen this position in the years to come. I think it quite possible, therefore, that the highly specialized activities of the members of our stock exchange, and particularly of our arbitrageurs, can render considerable support to this development.

In conclusion I would call your attention to the growing tendency in the last few years towards the broadening of stock ownership. The tendency is not confined to this country. Also elsewhere steps are being taken to make the small saver benefit from the possible advantages of an investment in securities. The post-war rise of the level of prosperity has been a strong incentive. Although much more could be said on the subject, it would carry me too far to enter into detail. I only wish to mention that the Amsterdam Stock Exchange in collaboration with some industrial companies and others has founded the "Stichting Verbreiding Effectenbezit" (Foundation for the broadening of stockownership), which is to be particularly engaged on studying these matters.

I have now come to the end of my address. I have tried to draw your attention to quite a number of aspects. Although I have only been able to sketch the outlines of the general set of problems, I hope that you have nevertheless received an impression of the position which the Amsterdam Stock Exchange occupies in the national economy of the Netherlands. I also hope that my words have convinced you that this old "mother of stock exchanges" has by no means lost her vitality.

I have no doubt but the future will, under new circumstances, offer to our Stock Exchange many opportunities to develop and strengthen her national and international position.

Today's Problems of Capital Exports

BY DR. KLAUS DOHRN

Member of the Board of Management of the Kreditanstalt für Wiederaufbau *(the Reconstruction Loan Corporation), of Frankfurt on Main, Germany*

The decade which is now beginning holds in store for the banks of Europe's leading industrial countries an important common task. This is to develop the traditional export financing methods, mainly designed as they were to ensure the rapid turnover of goods or to earn foreign exchange, into a system for long-term financing of the export of capital goods.

For this there are a number of reasons, among which those of a political nature concern us here only incidentally. The most important of the reasons which do now concern us appears to me to lie in the economic situation in which all the industrial countries of Europe nowadays find themselves, with certain differences of degree – a situation which in many respects resembles that at the end of the last century. The age of increased export of industrial and financial capital which then began was most visibly reflected in the building and financing of the great railroads across North America, through the wide expanses of Russia or in the Middle and the Far East. A unique system was then evolved for opening up the economies of under-developed areas, while keeping balances of payments in all-round equilibrium. The fact that in the creditor countries such equilibrium was achieved through capital exports meant that their export surplus, which stabilised their internal business cycle, did not need to be paid for – as we should nowadays say – by "importing inflation." In the debtor countries, on the other hand, the balance of payments was squared through *imports* of capital; and this meant that, in respect of the invested capital, no strains arose as between internal redemption and external transfer. Favourable conditions were thus created for obtaining a proper return on the capital projects then undertaken, depending as they did on repayment over a lengthy period.

You all know the basis on which that system rested. It was the fact that the great European stock exchange centres at that time had grown together into a homogeneous financial market, the functioning of which was not seriously hampered by either national or monetary frontiers. But the gateway to that common financial money market lay through the banks. The leading issuing houses of the day, acting singly or in syndicates, used just the right financing technique for each case. They fixed both the terms for each loan and the period to maturity so that the machinery would work smoothly. This meant that the timing had to be properly harmonized as regards the manufacture of the goods, the provision of the money for the borrower and the operation of the sinking fund.

The change in political and economic conditions after the first world war killed these delicately developed methods. It did so even though they were uniquely capable of reconciling the opposing interests and differing needs as between the supplying and receiving countries, and between the exporters of real and those of monetary capital, and although they were good for trade without being monetarily harmful. Quite rightly, therefore, it has become the custom to describe these forms of international capital movements as classical or traditional.

During the unhappy period between the two world wars the European industrial economies did not settle down. At that time it was necessary in turn to fight inflation, to check crises, and to carry out distended full-employment programmes. So countries had to screen themselves off in an effort to become independent of their balance of payments. That is why they had to abandon the gold standard, and in many cases even to impose exchange control. It was in this climate that they worked out the system which we have since known for financing exports by granting credit to exporters, mostly at medium terms. Exports became a tool of governmental policy for the purpose of procuring foreign exchange. In such conditions a method of export financing which was independent of the balance of payments situation was devised. In terms of financing technique the transfer of capital for the benefit of foreigners was transformed into the providing of quasi-internal credit.

After the second world war there was at first little change in these respects. Not until the middle of the fifties did our continent begin to get back into its old position as an exporter serving world markets. This process was typical of all the European industrial countries. But a particularly instructive example of what happened can be seen in Germany, which, having lost more than a third of its former home market, was forced more and more to export. As late as 1950 Western Germany's exports amounted to only just one half of its annual capital expenditure at home. Since then the value of its exports has overtaken that of such capital expenditure. Western Germany's exports of goods and services have increased fivefold since 1950, rising from DM 12 billion to DM 62 billion. Yet the Federal Republic represents not an exceptional but merely an extreme instance of the position in which all West European industrial countries now basically find themselves. By comparison with the United States all of them together have at their disposal only a relatively small internal market as measured by their total production capacity. That will be so even if, one day, the Common Market, the Free Trade Area and some kind of tariff bridge between the two become a reality. Hence the more these countries' national product grows, the more of their current production and investment they must export; and the exports in question will of course go mainly to those countries where such goods and capital find their market. That means nowadays, just as it did at the beginning of the present century, the developing countries. True, the geographical destination has changed, inasmuch as North America, Russia and the colonial territories have had their places taken by politically independent countries in Asia, Africa and Latin America. What has also above all changed, and changed with consequences highly adverse to any revival of the traditional forms for financing capital exports, is the world's political structure. One aspect of that change is the retirement of the colonial powers from the scene, together with their respective areas of more or less uniform law and currency. Another, more fundamental, is the undermining of concepts of law and property in international dealings, with the consequent great increase of the political risk entailed by international financing transactions.

There is yet another aspect, which I might describe as the "rediscovery of the balance of payments." At the end of 1958 the countries now united in the European Monetary Agreement joined in making their currencies externally convertible. Since then, in the words of the great Austrian economist Böhm-Bawerk, the balance of payments has again been giving the orders; as he would say, "the balance of trade obeys, not vice versa." Anybody who now tries in Western Europe to govern against his balance of payments by forcing his export surpluses – or allowing them to grow – without at the same time ensuring their proper financing, will get into conflicts which are hard to resolve. So will anybody who raises the official discount rate against the orders of the balance of payments, as the German Central Bank has unfortunately been doing, although of course it has to do so on cogent grounds of internal currency stability. That is why export financing, which for the reasons indicated will become more and more important, must be conducted in a manner conforming to the balance of payments more than hitherto. This means however that we in Western Europe are in principle once again facing a problem similar to the one at the turn of the century. Once again we have to finance a substantial part of our exports in a way which does no inflationary damage in the industrial exporting countries; nor must it cause excessive pressure on the monetary reserves in the developing importing countries, and so generate intolerable transfer difficulties. The essential difference between our present situation and the conditions 60 to 70 years ago is of course that at the moment we are without the common financing instrument available in that classic period. I mean of course an international capital market which is able and willing to act, and from which the funds required for the solution of our great problems of capital exporting could be drawn. That is why we have to look for other solutions of the problem of how to find the necessary funds for financing purposes.

After this glance – essential, in my opinion – at the general considerations, the following practical questions arise:

(1) What is nowadays the banks' proper place in the financing of capital exports from the industrial countries to the countries which are now being newly industrialized?

(2) Can banks, which work on borrowed money and therefore have to ask their debtors to provide them with liquidity, a fair return and security, cooperate at all in the financing of capital

exports when – as will frequently be the case in present-day circumstances – these things cannot be satisfactorily provided?

As to the first question I would say that capital projects, especially those of great size at new places with unexplored market conditions, require thorough analysis as regards the possibilities and forms of the financing entailed thereby. They also require, as a precondition for this, investigation of their long-term profitability. At this point the critical common sense of banking investigation methods has its proper place as a corrective offset to thinking merely in terms of engineering, to the sheer self-interest of sellers and to political motives of the most varied kinds. It would be unfortunate for the countries which provide capital and for those which receive it, and also a needless surrender of the Western world's business methods, if the financing and therefore the steering of the prospective large capital exports to the so-called underdeveloped countries fell completely into the hands of Government departments, and if decisions on such questions therefore became mainly dependent on politics and on rigid governmental budgetary practice. It must of course be clearly recognized that in view of the economic, social and political facts existing in the present-day world it will often be difficult, or even impossible, for banks to accept the full risk entailed by commitments of unknown duration in foreign countries where legal conditions are uncertain. But that must not and need not mean excluding the banks, with their experience, their critical judgment and their financing technique, from the practical handling of such great problems. These considerations bring us to our second question.

The answer to that second question has already been virtually anticipated in what I have so far said. Of course there is a wide field open for the banks to cooperate just in the sense that I described a moment ago. In all cases of capital projects where the return can be measured by the particular project itself, so that banking principles can be applied, it seems to me that financing through bank credit is possible. True, the profitability of investments in the so-called infrastructure, for instance in land improvement, irrigation, communications, schools and the like, cannot usually be so measured. Such investments are therefore in principle not suitable for bank credits. Instead, they must in the main be reserved for financing from official sources, either out of the budgets of the countries concerned or by way of loans from foreign Governments. Failing low interest rates and particularly long periods of maturity, however, infrastructure investments cannot as a rule be financed in a way which makes sense – unless indeed kind donors make for such purposes actual gifts of the kind which, as we all remember, the United States for years provided on so great a scale. Even in Europe the Governments will in future probably have to get more used to the idea of granting loans at particularly low interest rates, and for exceptionally long periods, to finance infrastructure projects in countries that wish to raise their neglected economic productivity. In many cases such projects will be required before conditions can be created in which commercial investments will pay, and before the financing of such investments on banking lines will be possible at all. At all events this indicates a sensible division of functions as between financing out of official monies on the one hand, and commercial financing through bank lending on the other. The question of how far money to finance such bank credits can be obtained from the capital markets, or from official funds, may be left open.

The most prominent example of how the problems of long-term investment financing can be solved even internationally in a manner that conforms to banking principles is, in my view, to be seen in the existence of the World Bank, and in the great success of its activity. It is no minimizing of the World Bank great achievements to say that of course neither it nor any other financing institutions charged with similar functions can alone solve the great international problems of capital export financing which will arise in future, especially in the relationship between the countries with long-standing industries and those now in course of development. The banking systems of Europe's surplus-exporting countries, which are interested in developing their economic relations with the countries that are building up new industries, seem to be just the ones which are called upon to make their own contribution in this field. The need for them to cooperate arises if only from the fact that every country must itself in some degree finance its own surpluses, and therefore in practice its capital exports. Apart from that such contributions by national banking systems would not only in a general way supplement the work of the World Bank and other international institutions of similar character, but could certainly in many cases also assume the form of close cooperation in individual projects. At all events we may assume that in the export of capital even in present circumstances there is and will continue to be enough room for financing by banks according to commercial criteria.

The third question, about the forms now suitable for the financing of capital exports, brings us to the heart of our problem.

I pointed out at the start that most countries have developed methods and institutions for financing capital exports by granting, to the exporters concerned, credits linked with the individual delivery contracts. As a rule, however, the limits of medium-term financing have not been exceeded. Such methods proved both expedient and useful as long as the economic policy objectives of promoting exports, and of obtaining foreign exchange, were in the foreground. My belief is that in future also the medium-term financing of the export of capital goods by this method of granting credit to exporters, and hence presupposing a supplier's credit, will continue on a large scale. In my view there can be no question of generally replacing these well-tried methods by others. What has to be done is to broaden the range by devising new financing methods, which shall conform better to certain financing requirements that are now arising and will in future arise more frequently. This applies in particular to the financing of large-scale plants and equipment. The increasing size which capital projects of this type are assuming abroad, especially in the developing countries, creates new problems in the field of financing. Let me at this point say a few words about the institutional problems connected with our subject.

As you know, for the purpose of export financing there are now in most countries special methods and special institutions, which in their activity are everywhere closely linked with the institutions handling export credit insurance. Without the protection conferred by these insurance institutions, generally organised on governmental lines, lenders nowadays – whether they are suppliers, banks, or individual firms setting up branches abroad – can no longer assume the great business risks and more particularly the immense political risks of foreign commitments. Under the protection of this spreading of risks through insurance various financing methods, which differ as between one country and another, are adopted. In the United Kingdom and Switzerland, apart from the British Commonwealth Development Association with its special functions, no institutions specializing in this field have yet appeared. In both countries the services of the traditional banking system are used in that connection. In the United Kingdom the special experience of its merchant bankers is available; so are their insurance schemes. In the case of Switzerland the country's exceptional wealth of capital, and the low interest rates in the Swiss capital market, greatly assist the financing of foreign investments. Other countries have developed special export-financing institutions, which present many differences as regards the procurement of their funds as well as in the methods by which they grant credit. Some of these specialized institutions, like the Banque Française pour le Commerce Extérieur in France or the Ausfuhrkredit AG in Germany, can resort – although in limited measure – to rediscounting at their Central Banks. For financing its business the German Ausfuhrkredit AG obtains funds at the same time from a rediscount line provided by the commercial banks which are its shareholders; to that extent therefore it obtains them from those banks' deposits, and hence in practice from the money market. Other institutions rely more on the capital market to provide funds for financing their business. Examples of this include the Istituto Mobiliare Italiano, the Mediobanca and the Efibanca in Italy, all of which have the backing of the Mediocredito. There is similar cooperation between the Export-Financiering Maatschappij and the Maatschappij tot Financiering van het Nationaal Herstel in the Netherlands. In Germany the Ausfuhrkredit AG confines itself to the financing of credits for medium terms of up to four years; it does so exclusively in the form of granting credit to the exporter. On the other hand the Kreditanstalt für Wiederaufbau, an official banking institution with Government connections, devotes itself to long-term export financing not only by granting credit to exporters but also – of late – by granting financial loans to foreign debtors. For the purpose of financing such loans the Kreditanstalt obtains funds partly by issuing long-term bonds or medium-term notes in the market, while it partly relies for that purpose on the resources of governmental funds for the promotion of capital exports, especially to the so-called under-developed countries. The varying character of the procedures is essentially due to differences between the national banking systems. But in no country, as it seems to me, have the specialized institutions become the sole agencies financing the export of capital goods. On the contrary, the traditional banking system everywhere cooperates in a great variety of ways to supplement the functions of the specialized institutions.

In the course of this cooperation, as I said before, new forms of financing have to be worked out. I hope that you will allow me to give you some practical examples of such new forms from the experience of my own work in Germany at the Kreditanstalt für Wiederaufbau, called in English the "Reconstruction Loan Corporation." Without any sacrifice of banking secrecy I shall try to describe to you some specimens of the credits which have recently been evolved in the course of our business practice.

The first example relates to financing the export of steelwork installations through a syndicate of engineering works. The period for which this financing runs is ten years. The picture presented by the assets side of the business is as follows:

Up to the expiry of the technical guarantee periods, that is for about three years, a credit is granted to the exporters concerned through the intermediary of their own bank, which guarantees them. After the expiry of these guarantee periods the exporters' bank is released from its guarantee; the credits then run, for the next four years, as direct loans to the exporters. Only from the eighth year onwards, that is during the last three years of the overall financing, are the remaining amounts of the credits previously granted to the exporters repaid. They are repaid out of a financial credit which the Kreditanstalt then grants to the foreign steelworks company, that is to the German supplying firms' customer, to enable it to pay the suppliers' remaining claims.

On the liabilities side of the transaction the Kreditanstalt during the first two years obtains funds from the resources of the guaranteeing bank; to that extent, therefore, it relies on resources of the money market. For the next eight years it finances the business either out of its own capital or out of funds which it procures in the capital market. In that connection it can if necessary obtain liquidity by falling back on a fund, to be formed by the Federal Government out of public monies, for the financing of development assistance schemes.

While the method here used is still a combination of financing the supplier and of granting a loan to the foreign debtor, the following examples comprise a number of variants of financial credits granted to foreign debtors.

Let me begin with a financial credit for DM 50 million, which was granted to finance a non-ferrous ore-working scheme and runs for 15 years. This credit is passed on to the ultimate debtor, an ore mining company, by a bank which specializes in long-term industrial financing in the country in question, a full guarantee being given by that bank. The debtor can use the credit only for certain capital purposes laid down in the loan contract. The financing is however done without any conditions being imposed as to the taking of German exports. On the contrary, the proceeds of the loan are at the debtor's free disposal; they could for instance also be used to finance the procurement of goods from countries other than Germany. As to the funds required for financing this business use is made, according to circumstances, either of the Kreditanstalt's own capital resources or of monies from the capital market.

A third version has been worked out in connection with the supply of power stations and their equipment to a Central American country. In this case the governmental investment bank of the country in question receives a 15-year loan, the proceeds of which are earmarked to finance capital projects of an electricity supply undertaking. The loan is granted in U.S. dollars and, since it is not expressed in the currency of the creditor's country, is at least theoretically subject to an additional currency risk. One-third of the loan proceeds is free from any requirement as to paying for German deliveries; it is used, more particularly, to finance the capital expenditure entailing payment in the local currency. The funds to finance this business also are obtained from various sources. Some come from the Kreditanstalt's own capital and reserves, some from the market. As regards a major portion of the amount of the loan it is also possible to have recourse to monies of the Government fund, previously mentioned, for developing countries.

The fourth example relates to the construction of a metallurgical work together with the appropriate roads, bridges and housing estates. The construction shall be done by a German supplying syndicate in cooperation with a British group; they share the whole project in the certain ratio of 2 : 1. In accordance with this formula the proportions delivered by the suppliers of the two countries are separately financed by credits of both suppliers respectively.

The debtor would be a metallurgical company, formed in the country concerned, and will receive a ten-year financial loan in DM. So far as this financial loan is intended to cover the laying out of roads, housing estates and bridges, the cooperating building firms will be paid out of it; the payments made to them include the outlays incurred by those firms in local currency on the building site. For the most part however the proceeds of the loan serve for purchase of the promissory notes which are to be delivered by the debtor to the suppliers according to the progress of construction.

In this case the funds for financing purposes are obtained during the first three years by the Kreditanstalt, which is the sole creditor in respect to the loan, from a banking syndicate associated with the supplying firms. Once again therefore, during an initial part of the total period covered by the financing, money market resources are used. Only after that use will be made in part of the Kreditanstalt's own resources, but in the main of monies from Government's funds.

Finally I should like to mention another financing scheme which we have worked out in connection with the participation in a project for the working of an ore deposit in an African country by an international ore mining company. In this case the contemplated DM loan to the mining enterprise is to be fitted as an integral part into a financing plan, in which provision is made not only for use of the enterprise's own capital resources, and of the DM loan, but also for bonded loans issued in the American market and for medium term-credits granted by American banks. An essential feature of this project, which is important for the development of the country concerned, is the assuring of a market for the greater part of the expected ore output; this is done through the fact that the interested metallurgical firms in U.S.A. and Germany undertake to purchase ore for a period of 20 years.

This is accordingly one of the rare cases in which the creditor countries will henceforth have, as a direct consequence of their previous capital exports, a prospect of a substantial increase in their imports and so for more earnings of foreign exchange by the ore producing countries.

The debtor will use the proceeds of the loan in full to finance the capital expenditure required for opening up the ore deposit; in this connection the debtor can use 40% of the loan proceeds freely, that is to say without any obligation to pay for deliveries from Germany. The finding of the funds to finance this 15-year loan for about DM 210 million is envisaged as follows:

The Kreditanstalt will obtain DM 160 million for periods of varying length from the German banking system, a substantial part being taken from institutions which by reason of their structure have relatively long-term deposits available. DM 50 million will be provided by the Kreditanstalt for the entire duration of the loan, with a possibility of recourse to the development fund. The tranches of credit to finance which are funds, initially obtained from banks only for medium periods will, on the expiry of these latter, be taken over for the rest of their life by a syndicate of the German steelworks interested in the ore deliveries. In the external relationship with the loan-debtor, however, the Kreditanstalt will be the sole creditor throughout the whole lifetime for which the transaction runs.

These various specimen credits, quoted by way of example, have three features in common:

(1) The credits are granted no longer to the exporter but, where possible and expedient, to foreign debtors, being granted either to the foreign importing customer himself, or to a foreign bank or to a foreign Government.

(2) All these credits are earmarked for the financing of capital projects on which the return that is to accrue from time to time can be calculated, and where it is possible to shape the terms of credit accordingly, especially as regards the periods to maturity.

(3) These credits are no longer entirely earmarked to pay for

exports, so that they are no longer – as we call it in my country-completely "earmarked for deliveries"; instead, they can at the debtor's option also be used to pay for deliveries from third countries or for outlays in his own national currency.

A feature not common to the examples here described, and to many other cases which I could not quote here, is the way in which funds are found to finance them. The method for doing this is flexibly adjusted to the possibilities from case to case, the funds being drawn from various sources, and often from several at the same time. In that connection the task of coordinating these various sources of finance falls no longer on the suppliers, as formerly, but on banking institutions.

After what I tried to say at the outset these various specimen credits will require no further exhaustive commentary. On the whole they represent a more or less successful effort to copy the pattern of traditional financing, so far as such financing is possible in present-day circumstances in my country. That is why it seems to me that the advantages offered by these specimens are essentialy those of the traditional method. As to this let me just say briefly:

The introduction of a grant of credit to the foreign debtor, instead of the previously predominant financing through the granting of credit to the exporting suppliers, helps us at the same time to solve two problems. In the first place the exporter can in this way be to a large extent relieved of his involuntary banker's function imposed on him by the previous system. He no longer needs to clutter up his balance sheet as much as before with long-term foreign claims. In certain circumstances, in view of the size of transactions in large-scale plants and equipment, this may be a point of importance for an industrial company's financing arrangements. Thus it meets certain desires which have long been entertained in industrial quarters.

Next, the use of quasi-bonded loan methods makes it more easily possible to adjust the financing of large projects, with repayment periods which by their nature are long, to the needs of the balance of payments situation. In the debtor countries it is thus possible to achieve better concordance between the internal finding of the monies for repaying the loan and the external transfer charge. If it further proved possible in future to finance creditor countries' capital exports more frequently in such ways, then two birds could be killed with one stone. First, it would be easier than before for the creditor countries to avoid the disadvantages of imported inflation; and secondly the debtor countries' balances of payments could at the same time be more readily relieved of short-term transfer liabilities.

Last, but not least, the relaxing or cancelling of the hitherto usual rule confining the credit granted to payment for exports would assist the building up of multilateral relations in international capital movements, and to that extent would counteract the so-called boomerang effect of capital exports where the borrower is required to take goods from the country providing the capital.

I must admit that as regards the method of procuring the funds the examples which I previously quoted differ from the traditional methods of financing through the capital market so much, so that advocates of conservative financing methods may find no cause for satisfaction. In many cases it is true that resources from the market, resources from public budgets, bank monies, liquid funds of industry, and funds borrowed for short, medium and long periods are thrown together into a single pool, where they then jointly provide funds to finance the granting of long-term loans.

Perhaps, however, we should not accept the present-day position in which capital exports, if left to themselves in the sense of depending solely on financing out of resources of private entrepreneurs or the capital market, will tend to go mainly to countries which are already developed and highly industrialized. It may be felt that on grounds of the most varied kind we ought to do something about this so as to ensure that such capital exports benefit also the developing countries, subject to the observance of commercial principles and on reasonable terms. If so, then at the moment the surplus countries will hardly get by without up-to-date methods for financing such business.

These few examples of how the funds required for financing such capital exports can be raised within the exporting country must certainly not be regarded as an ideal solution. They merely point to the direction in which our experiments must move. They all have in common two principles, namely that of mixing and that of breaking up.

The monies coming from the various lenders who cooperate in finding funds to finance the individual lending transactions are mixed together; and the periods for which monies are raised for alternating use in financing the grant of a long-term loan are broken up. I must not fail to point out one difficulty which arises in connection with this procedure for finding funds to finance the business.

Between the time when major capital projects are technically and financially prepared and that when the finance is required, which latter will not be until the projects are carried out, there are intervals of greater or lesser duration. Yet the financing of such projects must be arranged in a way which is binding on the bank or banks concerned before work can begin in the designing offices, at the factories and on the building sites. It is for that reason, and because the costs of procuring funds form an important component of the price quoted in every tender, that lenders often have to commit themselves for years in advance as regards both the amounts and the rates of interest. This of course entails risks, if for the obtaining of funds to finance such credits one has to rely not only on capital market sources but also on the money market, with its much greater fluctuations. At least in the circumstances now prevailing in my country such risks can be evened out only through a mixture with monies the terms for which are within certain limits independent of the market, that is with public monies. Without carrying these ideas any further I just wanted to point out this important function which may fall on officially formed funds with a view to finding, within the country, the capital which is to be exported.

I have confined myself to putting before you a few general thoughts about present-day problems of capital export, illustrating them by some typical examples from my own day-to-day activity.

Various Financial Aspects of the European Economic Community

By Jonkheer E. van Lennep
Treasurer-General of the Dutch Ministry of Finance

(1) HISTORICAL BACKGROUND

To get a clear picture of the problems with which the monetary authorities of the Common Market countries are confronted it is perhaps useful to start with a short review of the developments which took place in the past.

Before World War I one could say that there was a high degree of integration of the national economies. That is to say the national economies were highly susceptible to outside influences because there were practically no obstacles to international movements of goods, services, capital and persons. The only exception consisted of the existence of import duties. The main task of the monetary authorities was to look after the evolution of the national economy in such a manner that the countries could meet their international financial obligations. This means that the most important, if not the only, target of monetary policy was to maintain the equilibrium of the balance of payments, to the extent that its equilibrium did not come about automatically. The often unpleasant effects for the internal economy, consisting of serious fluctuations in national income, employment and prices, were taken for granted.

During the interwar period resistance was growing against this carrying away on the waves of the international business cycle. The authorities felt themselves more and more responsible for internal economic developments, especially for the preservation of a high employment level.

Two sorts of instruments were used:

(a) Restrictions on importing goods and services to bring about a direct shift from foreign to domestic production.

(b) Measures to raise internal demand for the purpose of stimulating domestic production, for example through promoting public works. Such a policy could lead to balance of payments deficits and therefore made the use of import restrictions a necessary addition of these measures.

In both cases the freedom of international trade and payments was limited in favour of domestic employment. However the advantages of a far reaching degree of an international division of labour, were thus abandoned.

After the last World War it was realized again that the advantages of an international division of labour should be utilized. In accordance with this idea several international organisations were established, for instance the I.M.F., the G.A.T.T., the O.E. E.C. and the Benelux.

However, the return to a maximum international division of labour through an unrestricted international flow of goods, services and capital was to be accomplished without interfering with the responsibility of the national authorities for the domestic economic developments, particularly with regard to employment and prices.

The responsibility for a high degree of employment, a stable price level and a balance of payments equilibrium, a prerequisite for maintaining the freedom of international payments, implies a three dimensional objective of economic policy, sometimes referred to as the "magic triangle."

(2) THE NECESSITY OF COORDINATION

The above-mentioned targets of economic policy have gradually been accepted by every country. At first sight one would be inclined to assume that in these circumstances the magic triangle presents the key for a harmonious economic development and that there is no need for an international coordination of economic policies. However it is not so simple. A closer examination of the magic triangle brings to light a number of problems which make international coordination desirable and even necessary. These problems result in short from:

(a) differences in interpretation concerning the targets of economic policy,

(b) differences of opinion on the order of priority of these targets,

(c) differences of opinion with regard to the instruments with which these targets can be materialized,

(d) difficulties arising from the fact that the targets of economic policy which were accepted in principle sometimes cannot be realized because of political circumstances.

I would like to make the following remarks to illustrate these just mentioned four points.

(a) Differences of interpretation

It may very well occur that the three policy objectives – price stability, high degree of employment and balance of payments equilibrium – are differently interpreted in one country than in another. Let us therefore review these three principles.

(i) price stability. Does this mean that prices ought to be constant in all circumstances? If so, is then for instance the consequence that price subsidies concerning rents and agricultural products may only be reduced when other prices decline? Which viewpoint must be taken regarding changes in prices caused by revisions in the rates of costprice increasing taxes? Can we leave these out of consideration or not? Or to mention another extreme case, can we simply say that we must examine the price level largely from the balance of payments viewpoint, in other words should we be satisfied if the domestic price level does not increase more than the average foreign price level?

(ii) high degree of employment. The ideas on this problem have been subjected to a drastic change in the course of the years. However, there exists by no means a uniformity in viewpoints on this problem. It is clear that the higher the employment level is which is pursued in a country, the greater is the danger of inflationary disturbances. Moreover, it is possible that under certain circumstances a difference in targets can result in a difference in policy. At the time of general economic expansion the country setting the lower target will be prepared at an earlier stage to introduce an anti-inflationary policy than the country which sets the higher target.

(iii) balance of payments equilibrium. Also in this respect is it possible to have different views. May I point out some examples of targets of balance of payments policy which all can be classified under the heading "balance of payments equilibrium."

– The balance of payments on current account is permitted to show a deficit on condition that this deficit is covered by foreign loans.

– The current account has to show at least a surplus sufficient to cover a high level of net capital exports; security transactions with foreign countries must be left out of consideration.

– When defining the balance of payments equilibrium all long-term capital movements must be included in the balance of payments.

– The balance of payments policy must take into account the necessity of a rise of the foreign exchange reserves equal to the rise in foreign trade or the rise in domestic liquidities.

(b) Which target of economic policy should eventually be given priority

One can imagine that a balance of payments equilibrium and a high degree of employment cannot be materialized simultaneously. This situation will appear in case of a world depression. Then policy makers should trie to reach agreement on the question whether the employment policy has to prevail over the policy aimed at maintaining a balance of payments equilibrium or not. In a period of excessive economic activity no difference of opinion may exist regarding the problem of priority of internal or external stability. Suppose that in such a period in certain countries with a balance of payments surplus the policy is directed more towards internal stability than towards external stability. These countries will then curb internal demand. This will on the one hand result in a decrease of the tightening of the labour market and in a lessening of the upward pressure on wages and prices, on the other hand however in a rise of the balance of payments surplus. This can result in balance of payments difficulties in other countries. These countries will also have to pursue a deflationary policy if they wish to counteract these difficulties. It is possible that ultimately this procedure will be the best; in doing so the conditions may be created for a combined attainment of the three targets of policy. However, it is just as well possible that in the long run it would have been better if the first-mentioned countries had not taken deflationary measures, but to a certain extent had allowed internal pressures to influence wages, prices and the balance of payments. Therefore an important argument for the coordination of economic policy is that differences of opinion about the question which one of the three targets should be given priority, should be prevented, in case the three policy aims cannot be materialized simultaneously.

(c) Disagreement concerning the instruments to be used

Particularly if pursuing not only the freedom of trade but also of capital movements coordination of the instruments of economic policy to be used is a prerequisite. Let us suppose that it is necessary to stem a threatening overexpansion of economic activity. An overexpansion means that investments surpass savings. There are two ways of restoring the balance, namely the level of investments can adapt itself to the level of savings, or, on the other hand, the level of savings is raised to such an extent that it equals the level of investments. When prefering the first solution the authorities need not do anything other than check credit creation. When the second solution is pursued, it will be necessary that the authorities enforce a curtailment of consumption, e.g. by reducing consumption of the public sector through cuts in the budget or of the private sector by raising costprice increasing taxes or public utility rates.

In the first case the interest rate will rise, while in the second case the interest rate will remain stable or even decline. This means, that if two countries follow different ways the result will be that there will be a movement of capital between them. This movement of capital does undermine the policies in both countries. In the country in which consumption was curtailed, the disequilibrium between savings and investments will tend to persist as savings will flow out to the neighbour country. In the other country the level of investments will increase through the availability not of additional national but of foreign savings. A lack of coordination would mean that no action can be taken by the authorities of either country at all.

(d) Difficulties to materialize the accepted economic target arising from political circumstances

Conducting a certain policy, accepted in itself as correct, is sometimes impossible through political difficulties, e.g. because pressure groups prevent the execution of such a policy. If, however, a recommendation of an international body has been put forward the authorities responsible for economic policy can take a firmer stand against these internal pressure groups.

This does not mean that coordination must always result in a formal recommendation to conduct a certain policy. The main point, however, is that a country explains its own policy before an international forum and that attention is paid to the possible criticism which other countries express. Of course, the representatives of the criticized country will often not be free in their reply to that criticism as

(a) many important policy decisions must be kept secret up to the last moment;

(b) as long as the government has not yet decided about a change of policy it is generally difficult for a representative of such a government to express in public that he is in favour of such a change of policy.

The representatives of the other countries naturally will have to limit their criticism to those policy aspects, which have international repercussions. Problems of internal distribution of income etc. should therefore be left out of consideration.

The word criticism must be understood to mean, not that one pretends to have a better insight about the most desirable economic policy than someone else, but that one hopes to put forward arguments which convince the other that the policy has to show more consideration for the interest of other countries. Generally a frank exchange of thoughts about all four mentioned groups of problems (interpretation of the policy targets, order of priority of the targets, selection of the instruments of economic policy, and the conflict between economic necessity and political difficulties to take certain measures) shall in the long run without doubt create an atmosphere where national ideas about the direction of policy will approach each other closely, and especially that the policy makers will take international implications more and more into account. In this respect it might be worthwhile to mention, that it is politically less difficult to use instruments of monetary policy as the discount rate etc. than other instruments. It is no wonder therefore that recommendations of international organisations often concentrate on the need to use other instruments of economic policy than the monetary policy.

(3) COORDINATION IN THE E.E.C.

Up to now I have spoken in a general theoretical sense about the promotion of the international division of labour and the related problem of the coordination of economic and financial policy. It is also in the E.E.C. that these aspects play a role, since the E.E.C. aims at the liberalization of international economic relations in order to arrive at the largest possible international division of labour. This shows that also in the framework of the E.E.C. it is regarded desirable to maintain a balance of payments equilibrium in order to secure the aforementioned liberalization. On the other hand, a number of autonomous governments are represented in E.E.C., which are responsible for the economic development of their own country.

All these aspects find their repercussions in the E.E.C. Treaty. Article 104 of this Treaty states: "Each Member State shall pursue the economic policy necessary to ensure the equilibrium of its overall balance of payments and to maintain confidence in its currency, while ensuring a high level of employment and the stability of the level of prices." Here we find again the three elements of the "magic triangle." In the first sentence of Article 105 the coordination of this policy is prescribed: "In order to facilitate the attainment of the objectives stated in Article 104, Member States shall coordinate their economic policies." In fact the problem of coordination in the E.E.C. does essentially not differ from the world-wide coordination problem which I pointed out in the first part of my speech. Yet there are certain points of difference.

Firstly, it can be put forward that the necessity of coordination in the E.E.C. presents itself more urgently than on the wider international level. The ties between the countries of the Community are far stronger than those between members of organizations covering a geographically wider area. This is first of all so because the removal of restrictions goes considerably further. With regard to the movement of goods there is not only the need to eliminate quantitative barriers, but also import duties. Furthermore, a customs union implies a common external tariff and a common external trade policy. Also in respect of the movement of services, persons and capital and the right of establishment of persons and enterprises in partner countries, a complete freedom has to be reached ultimately. No larger international organisation has ever put this forward as its target. This greater degree of integration means that possible disturbances in the member countries affect the economies of the partner countries to a stronger extent. The interest one has in a correct policy in the partner countries is therefore bigger. Likewise, the interest one has in the correctness of its own policy increases also as the freedom of the international movements grows, because a wrong policy shall have a stronger influence on the balance of payments. Just the fact of the existence of an organisation like the E.E.C. has already a psychological influence on the private sector. The enterpreneurs do not consider the partner countries any longer as foreign countries in the normal sense. Their advertisements, their production schemes, in one word their entire conduct is based on the fact that the E.E.C. countries form a common market. The responsibility to prevent breaches in this market therefore increases.

After all the governments have also an interest in the unhampered continuation of the E.E.C. On the one hand, large financial sacrifices have been made on behalf of the Community. Large amounts are put into the Development Fund for Overseas Territories and into the European Investment Bank: through the European Social Fund the expense for occupational re-training and resettlement of workers in the six countries is carried jointly. On the other hand the E.E.C. causes in many fields a strong change of national policies.

Because of these reasons the E.E.C. gives an additional inducement to bring about a farreaching coordination of economic and financial policies. A fortunate circumstance is the fact that a further reaching coordination is also possible. For it concerns a limited number of countries; moreover, their economic structure shows a rather large similarity. The limitedness of the number of countries presents the possibility that officials of the six countries who have a direct responsibility for the preparation of policy in their own country, meet each other often and thoroughly discuss at these meetings developments in member countries.

The institutional framework of the E.E.C. is also favorable for the realization of coordination. The European Commission is charged through article 103 of the Treaty to make proposals regarding economic policy to the Council of Ministers, which after that can decide on the measures appropriate to the situation. This task of the European Commission which is a body independent of the Governments creates the possibility to effect a truly "European" vision on cyclical problems. Moreover, the Community possesses in certain circumstances a certain means of pressure for forcing a country to pursue a certain policy. This is namely the case when a country which has balance of payments difficulties either requests so-called mutual assistance, or makes an appeal on escape clauses. In both cases the Community can agree to these requests on condition that a certain policy is pursued.

One of the bodies, which play an important part in the problem of coordination is the Monetary Committee. This Committee is established under Article 105 of the Treaty and consists of officials of the governments and of the central banks, who are directly concerned with the determination of policy in their own country. The members act in this Committee as independent experts, which greatly promotes the frankness of the discussions and the impact of the various opinions.

At least twice a year this Committee submits the development in each of the member countries to a profound investigation. These examinations result in reports to the European Commission and to the Council of Ministers. These reports are confidential which also promotes the frankness of the discussions. In addition the Monetary Committee studies, on its own initiative or at the request of the Commission or the Council, other problems in the monetary or financial sector, which problems are of importance to the Community.

Besides the Monetary Committee an Economic Policy Committee has been established some time ago. This Committee is also composed of high officials of the governments and the central bank, but in this instance as government representatives. The sessions are less frequent than those of the Monetary Committee.

(4) ACTIVITIES OF THE MONETARY COMMITTEE

The activities of this Committee are entirely in line with the problems mentioned in the first part of my speech. Its aim is to specify the three principles of economic policy and to determine the relative weight which has to be given in certain circumstances to each of them. Another very important problem which faces the Monetary Committee is the choice of instruments to be used.

It is clear that it is not in all cases recommendable to use purely monetary instruments. Notwithstanding its name the Monetary Committee has already declared more than once that other than monetary instruments should be used, for influencing total demand, e.g. the budget and the control on activities in the building sector. Experience shows however that some countries of the E.E.C. have only a limited arsenal at their disposal. One of the tasks of coordination shall be to build up gradually such a collection of instruments that the national economies become as flexible as necessary to meet the high requirements which the Common Market demands regarding the realization of the three elementary policy principles.

The experience in the Monetary Committee has furthermore proved that a really justified recommendation of a certain choice of instruments of economic policy is only possible if a clear and also comparable picture of factual developments can be formed.

In this field a lot of work still has to be done. I would like to mention particularly the monetary analysis. Between the Member-States of the E.E.C. such institutional differences exist that a statistical comparison of monetary developments is at the moment very difficult.

A second sort of analysis indispensable for a just interpretation of these developments is an analysis of the various government budgets. Several budget items, concerning expense as well as revenue, have a different influence on economic developments. It is therefore very expedient to have a uniform classification of these items at the disposal. Further, it is necessary to reach a uniform viewpoint about the monetary effect of the different methods of financing.

A proper monetary analysis and a budgetary comparison are

needed for the activities of the Monetary Committee. Therefore it is to be welcomed that these aspects are studied by the European Commission.

(5) THE CAPITAL MOVEMENTS IN THE E.E.C.

As we are discussing the tasks of the Monetary Committee I would like to invite your attention at this point for a matter which is not directly concerned with the field of coordination, but which is very closely coupled with that problem, namely the liberalisation of capital movements. As I already mentioned, the E.E.C. Treaty prescribes the liberalization of capital movements; this I put forward as one of the reasons that in the E.E.C. a more intensive coordination is needed than in other international organizations. It is the duty of the Council of Ministers of the E.E.C., acting on a proposal of the European Commission, to draw up the directives which will gradually lead to this freedom.

One can persist that all capital movements promote the functioning of the common market as all capital movements stimulate the international division of labour. This however is still theory as for the time being there are in fact such differences between the six countries, in policy as well as in institutional circumstances, that surely not every capital movement leads to a greater yield of that capital for the community as a whole.

I underlined already the necessity of coordination of economic and financial policies if one wishes to achieve a general and lasting freedom of international economic relations. At this moment this coordination is not at all perfect which, with regard to the liberalization of capital movements urges caution. I would like to mention in this respect the recent German measures in the field of monetary policy, which already compelled Germany itself to take defensive measures to counteract undesirable external repercussions, which measures partly contain a limitation of the freedom of capital movements. When full freedom of capital movements had existed the German measures could have had certain undesirable results for the partner countries as well as for Germany itself. For the partner countries because a loss of foreign exchange reserves could have resulted from the German measures. For Germany itself because the resulting inflow of foreign liquidities would have undermined its policy of diminishing the liquidity of the banks, which would have made unattainable the final goal of this policy, namely the limitation of credit expansion.

On the ground of the still existing lack of coordination it has not yet been possible to realize the complete liberalization of capital movements. On the other hand, some capital transactions ore so closely linked with for instance the movement of goods or with the freedom of establishment and the movement of persons that a ban on these capital transactions would also restrict the freedom of these categories. As such can be named direct investments, capital transfers in the personal sector and credits concerning the supply of goods.

The first directives, which were issued recently, are based on these considerations. The freed capital movements are in general limited to transactions, which are closely coupled with the other sectors. An additional liberalization of capital movements needs before hand a further improvement of the coordination of economic and financial policy. To prevent any misunderstanding I wish to point out that liberalization means in this respect the unconditional acceptance of the obligation to set free the transactions in question. Naturally this does not mean that one does not grant a greater freedom if and as long as the circumstances permit. The actual freedom of capital movements within E.E.C. is nowadays greater than the obligations one has undertaken.

The question could be put forward if the procedure should not have been reversed, that is to say that capital movements should have been set free whereafter the necessity of coordination would have arisen automatically. This is also the case with regard to the liberalization of goods and services. The Treaty dictates liberalization of these categories independently of a preceding realization of coordination. Could not the same line of conduct have been decided upon regarding the capital movements?

It is my opinion that this question has to be answered in the negative. Liberalization of goods and services in general requires that the target of the external equilibrium is maintained in whatever manner. The authorities have some freedom regarding the timing of action and the choice of instruments. The liberalization of capital movements, however, demands a greater degree of cooperation between all member countries, also with respect to the moment of action and the instruments to be used. If sufficient advance coordination is lacking, freedom of capital movements would certainly not fail to bring about a certain harmonisation of policies, but this would tend to be a policy of high interest rates, which is not necessarily identical with a policy of a high rate of savings and investments.

Let me conclude this chapter by mentioning the position of the security transactions. Certain circumstances, e.g. international political tensions, can suddenly cause very great shifts in international payments. This could result in such a heavy burden on the foreign exchange reserves that one can be compelled to limit the freedom in this field but also in the sector of goods and services. It may therefore be desirable to guide payments linked with security transactions through a separate channel, which under normal conditions has an open communication with the usual channels, but which can be detached in special circumstances. The E.E.C. regulations for liberalization concerning capital movements have taken this desirability into account and have allowed for the existence of the free currency market for security transactions.

(6) EVALUATION OF THE COORDINATION IN THE E.E.C.

Let us try to come now to an evaluation of the question how far the coordination of economic policy is working satisfactorily in practice.

It is thereby useful to keep clearly in view which demands may be reasonably set for this coordination. The opinion is often heard, that the monetary provisions represent the weakest part of the Rome Treaty. Those who hold that opinion, assert that these provisions are based to a much too large extent on the full maintenance of sovereignty of the member countries in the financial and monetary sector. They regard it unsatisfactory that the monetary provisions of the Rome Treaty do not offer an absolute guarantee that the Common Market will never be frustrated by balance of payments difficulties of member countries. They state that notwithstanding all beautiful provisions on coordination, monetary committee, recommendations, mutual assistance etc. sooner or later the freedom of economic relations within the Community will be impaired for some time by serious inflationary disturbances in one or more member countries.

Let us for argument's sake suppose for a moment that there is a well-founded reason for pessimism. But, one can ask, which regulations in the monetary field should then have been made?

Several replies to that question can be found in economic literature. I will mention some examples:

(a) One European currency must be created.

(b) A monetary fund must be created in which the foreign exchange reserves of member countries are to be deposited in full or in part.

(c) The Monetary Committee must receive supra-national authority in the field of monetary policy.

I will make some remarks about these suggestions.

I would like to leave out the idea of one European currency. It is clear to every expert that a common currency cannot be the beginning but solely the symbolic final stone of a political federation. The problem of the coordination of economic policy is by no means eliminated or resolved by a common currency. On the contrary, the problem of coordination would be aggravated.

With regard to the creation of a monetary fund I should like to make the following comment. A real guarantee that member countries will never invoke the escape clauses, can only be obtained if this fund would be able to grant credits to an unlimited extent, that means, if the member countries, which have no balance of payments difficulties, are prepared to make unlimited contributions. It is clear that this willingness can never be anticipated. Suppose that those other countries have an overall balance of payments equilibrium, which may be composed of a surplus on the deficit country and deficits towards third countries. An unlimited granting of credits to the deficit country would mean that the foreign exchange reserves of the partners decline. Besides, this would mean that an inflation, which causes the deficits, also has an unhampered impact in the partner countries. By so doing the external value of the currency not only of the inflation country but also of the currencies of the other countries would be endangered. It is to be prevented that for the sake of the freedom of economic relations within the Community the freedom of economic relations with the rest of the world is imperilled unnecessarily.

A fund too would only be able to grant credits on a limited scale and then only on the condition that the country pursues a certain policy. For this task, however, we do not need a fund. A limited granting of credits by the member countries is already covered by the Treaty. Furthermore, a disavantage of the creation of a fund is that it gives the impression of being more or less entitled to assistance, which diminishes the necessity of taking unpleasant corrective measures in due time.

Finally, the suggestion of reinforcing the authority of the Monetary Committee. Those who advocate this solution, often mention as an example the Federal Reserve System of the United States. It appears however that the supporters of this idea make a mistake when believing that inflationary disturbances are excluded, if only one can centrally direct the policy of the central banks with regard to the granting of credits to the treasuries, the discount rate, etc. The central banks are not able to check every increase in the volume of money, particularly not when this is the effect of a balance of payments surplus or of dishoarding of liquidities. In these cases it is up to governments to exert a counteracting influence through taxes, loans and expenditures. Furthermore, central banks are not able to take effective action against an excessive cost inflation and an excessive building activity, as I stated before.

In so far as one believes in eliminating the possibility of balance of payments deficits by rendering greater authority to the Monetary Committee, it is therefore my opinion that this is based on an overestimation of the importance of the instruments of monetary policy.

If one thinks however that supra-national powers should be granted to the Monetary Committee with regard to all instruments of economic policy, then one advocates in fact one federal European Government. However, in that case we have exceeded the limits of political reality, and we must not lose sight of this reality. It is technically impossible to forge the six Common Market countries into one economic entity at short notice. From a political point of view too it is impossible to hand over authorities to a supra-national body, which up till now belong to national authorities, especially in the delicate field of the control of economic activities. I even wonder whether politically speaking this would be desirable. The success of the policy of the authorities depends largely on the behaviour of the different groups of the population. Would the population not show a greater measure of adherence in the case of policy established by their authorities than when this policy is determined by a central body of the Community? For the time being I believe this question must be answered in the affirmative. The public is still too little interested and involved in the governing bodies of the E.E.C. In this situation the Community can perform behind the scenes a much more useful task as a "European pressure group" than as an institution which itself determines the economic policy.

I do not want to pretend that in the E.E.C. the present state of affairs regarding the coordination of the monetary, financial and economic policies leaves nothing to be desired. Nevertheless, my general judgement is certainly positive. Institutionally the framework exists for a thorough deliberation about all problems of importance. The Monetary Committee studies and advises. The European Commission gives independant, virtually European, advices to the governments concerned and is assisted in this field by the Economic Policy Committee. The reports of the Monetary Committee are forwarded as confidential documents to the national authorities. It is important for the necessary political follow-up of the recommendations of the E.E.C.-Commission and the Monetary Committee, that the Ministers of Finance of the six countries meet regularly in the presence of members of the E.E.C.-Commission as well as of the presidents of the Monetary Committee and the Economic Policy Committee.

Those who are officially and actively concerned in this field would sometimes desire that their work would meet with a wider reponse on the political level. On the other hand more than once the responsible ministers will be of opinion that the technical advices do not take the political reality adquately into account. With regard to all these difficulties we should not forget, however, that the present experience only covers the relatively short period of $2\frac{1}{2}$ years. In my opinion the most important fact is that all working in this field, the Ministers, the European Commission, and the national civil servants, are convinced that they are constructively engaged in developing quite a new dynamic force in this field, which is so vital for the success of the E.E.C.

(7) THE EXTERNAL FINANCIAL ASPECTS OF THE COMMUNITY

The question arises how the relationship of the Community with the outer world will develop as the uniformity of the economic and financial policy of the six countries grows. Will this uniformity not lead to a policy, that deviates in such a way from that of the outer world, that in the end the E.E.C. will form a closed bloc. This question is the more obvious as there are already difficulties in the trade policy sector, as evidenced by the conflicts between the E.E.C.and the European Free Trade Area.

The existence of the latter difficulties logically results from the existence of the E.E.C. as a customs union. As a matter of definition this union means discrimination in the trade field towards third countries. In the monetary field however it is by no means certain that such difficulties will ever arise.

Putting it first and foremost that for the time being there are no frictions in this sphere. In the international contact between the monetary authorities of the E.E.C.-countries and third countries, e.g. in the framework of the I.M.F. or the B.I.S., there are no conflicts at all. Yet the question whether in the future difficulties may ever arise merits our attention.

In the beginning of my lecture I have tried to point out that a certain worldwide coordination of economic and financial policy of the national authorities must take place, if one desires to secure on the largest possible scale the international division of labour. Thereafter, however, I have pointed out too that in the E.E.C. this coordination will have to take place more intensively and will moreover be achieved more easely. The latter would lead to the six countries taking a common decision as to the priority of the three mentioned aims of policy, if the world situation is such that these aims cannot be materialized simultaneously. If, for instance during an international depression, the unanimous choice would fall on the priority of the internal equilibrium this means a balance of payments deficit of the six countries, which in the long run could lead to a seclusion of the Community from the outer world.

In this case a conflict would arise between the E.E.C. and the outer world, which conflict would have its source in a monetary controversy. I should like to discuss for a moment the question whether this seclusion is in accordance with the international treaties of a wider nature. The G.A.T.T. recognises the possibility that the members of a customs union use import restrictions against third countries without applying them to their partners. The I.M.F. to the contrary does not make provision for that possibility, at any rate not in its articles of agreement. That is not to say that the possibility could not be created. The I.M.F. is qualified to allow certain balance of payments restrictions if there are special reasons, particularly balance of payments difficulties. This allowance may contain at the same time the permission to apply these restrictions in a discriminatory way. So there is no certainty about the latter permission but the possibility does exist.

Another question is, however, whether it is probable that there will ever be such monetary controversies that they will lead to a seclusion of the Common Market from the outer world. I said in the beginning already that after the war the idea has grown that one had to strive after an internal as well as an external equilibrium at the same time and that with this idea the necessity of coordination has also been recognized on a world wide scale. This idea has again exercised a strong influence in the framework of the present activities aiming at the reorganization of the O.E.E.C. In the reorganised O.E.E.C., namely the Organisation for Economic Cooperation and Development more emphasis will be put on the coordination of economic policies. It is important that the United States and Canada will also be included in this framework. The stronger the coordination will grow on a world wide scale the smaller the probability of conflicts between the E.E.C. and the rest of the world will be.

Furthermore it is clear that it would not be desirable that the E.E.C. goes into a certain seclusion from the outer world. For in such a situation the aim, promotion of the international division of labour, would be frustrated. The E.E.C. only turns out an essential contribution towards this if it combines the internal liberalization with the largest possible external freedom. The

E.E.C.-partners and the European Commission have repeatedly given evidence of this liberal mind.

For all these reasons I think that we can be optimistic with regard to the danger of a conflict in the field of the monetary policies between the E.E.C.-countries and the outer world. This does not alter the fact that existence of a potential conflict cannot be denied.

But on the other hand I wish to emphasize the positive aspects of the E.E.C. The Community contributes to an important degree to the so strongly desired increase of the monetary and economic discipline in the world. In so far as this greater discipline leads to the formation of a separate bloc the monetary expert must – as I said before – be suspicious of it and should try to avoid this detrimental side as much as possible. However, in sofar as this greater discipline leads to a further reduction of the diversity in the financial and economic policy of the various countries, we can only welcome the establishment of the Community. This means then that the Community has also brought a new dynamic force in the framework of world wide cooperation, which can only lead to a further perfection of the final goal, namely the realization of the "magic triangle" and the promotion of the international division of labour.

Medium Term Credits from the Monetary Point of View

BY PROFESSOR S. POSTHUMA
Managing Director of De Nederlandsche Bank N.V.

To ask questions about the monetary aspects of medium-term credits means in practice that one has in mind the danger that expansion of this form of lending may lead to monetary disturbances. Such disturbances may on the one hand result from a shift within a given total amount of credit, so that an increase of medium-term lending would mean a decrease of credit already existing in other forms. On the other hand one may be thinking of an expansion which does not entail a mere shift but rather an enlargement of the total volume of credit.

Although even the first possibility may have monetary implications, these are on a different plane from those in the latter case. Of course in both cases the first question to ask is whether there is any need for medium-term credit to expand. But if one accepts that there is, then the problems connected with any shift within a more or less fixed total volume of credit will primarily relate to matters of business organization, or they may perhaps be of a social character. Monetary problems will arise in that connection only in the last instance.

In the second case we are primarily concerned with a monetary problem. But we live in an expanding economy, and an increase of the total real national product in conditions of balanced growth generally also requires expansion of the whole money and credit mechanism; in a certain sense, indeed, it depends on such expansion. That is why the enlargement of a specific *form* of credit, even though it may be accompanied by an increase of the total credit outstanding, need not in itself cause uneasiness. Here therefore the question of what monetary aspects are inherent in an expansion of credit at medium term merges into the much wider one of what is the optimum relation between an increase in the volume of money and credit as a whole, on the one hand, and the economic expansion in real terms on the other.

The subject which I have been assigned for discussion at this meeting is therefore limited on two sides. On the one side it excludes the problems of business organization which may result from shifts within the country's existing credit structure; such problems may arise both in institutions the continued existence of which is thereby threatened, and in those which expand their medium-term lending to a more than proportionate extent, or start to devote themselves especially to that form of lending. On the other side we can disregard the fundamental question of how great an increase of credit is needed in order to realize optimum real expansion.

Inside the field thus defined our principal question will be to what extent an increase of medium-term lending by particular institutions must be regarded as mainly a matter of transmitting credit or as one of creating purchasing power. Since however in different countries institutions with the same sort of names (and often to outward appearance even of very similar structure) diverge considerably as regards the nature of their activities, my observations will have to be somewhat abstract in character. I shall in many cases have to leave it to my audience to work out for themselves what the applying of those observations to the actual facts in their own country would mean.

In concrete terms they must work out whether, in the event of an increase in lending by a particular institution, there is broad agreement between the period for which monies lent may be regarded as recoverable and the period within which the institutions creditors intend to use this money themselves. Is there equilibrium from that point of view, or is there a latent strain? Since this is not a legal but an economic problem, that question cannot be answered by reference to the periods legally fixed. As regards the possibilities of repayment of the monies lent the individual debtor can to a certain extent rely on the possible substitution of creditors; macro-economically, however, a credit taken has become a fixed credit as from the time at which it has produced in the total economic circulation an expansion which cannot be reversed without disturbances. As regards the liabilities to repay deposits and borrowed monies the institution transmitting the credit needs take no account of the behaviour of individual creditors; it needs pay attention only to their behaviour as a body, changes in the composition of that body through substitution of account-holders being disregarded. If in that sense there is equality between debtors and creditors, then there is prima facie no monetary problem. If there is not such equality, or in other words if the increase of credit is financed through a rise in the deposits (of whatever kind) of third parties, who in their own plans for expenditure include those deposits as potential payment media, then the expanding of credit implies creation of purchasing power. The same applies if the bank finances an expansion of its lendings out of a surplus of its own liquid assets, so far as that surplus arises from past lending activities and not from a synchronized increase of its capital resources either through retention of profit or through attraction of new capital.

Hence in this connection savings mean every transfer of purchasing power available to a credit-transmitting institution, so far as that purchasing power has been derived from current income and not from the turning of capital assets into money, nor from the withdrawal of money from hoardings.

Effective creation of purchasing power takes place on every increase of lending by institutions whose liabilities to outside parties increase pari passu, in so far as these liabilities are virtually regarded by the creditor as liquid assets. Here I deliberately do not use the term "money," because that involves the risk of obscuring a process which may be important in this connection. A flow of income which is turned into claims which have not quite the character of money, but which the creditor can nevertheless turn into money at will on relatively short notice and practically without cost, may affect the creditor's actions as a spender in exactly the same way as if he had kept this money on current account instead of putting it on a time deposit or on some sort of savings account. The point is, that a flow of income which is turned into an account with a credit granting institution can create at the same moment two flows of orders for goods and services; on the one hand by the borrower and on the other hand by the holder of the account, even if drawings on this account are subject to some form of notification, since he knows that the actual payment of his orders will only fall due at a future date.

The question to what extent the creation of purchasing power is justifiable from the point of view of a country's economy is a separate one, which I may here disregard.

So far as an increase of liquidity is indispensable for, or leads to, enlargement of the national product in real terms it does not cause disturbance, but is to be considered a condition for the maintaining of monetary equilibrium. Since it is, however, always possible that an increase of total bank credit – implying liquidity creation – exceeds the possible real expansion, and as such being economically unjustifiable, the monetary authorities have in principle a task here. In order to be able properly to carry out that task they must be in a position to adopt measures for influencing, through the private credit mechanism, the creation of purchasing power.

One possible such measure would be themselves to act either as lender or as borrower. In addition they have power to impose restrictions on lending and borrowing by certain private institutions which engage in such pursuits. That applies in particular to what are called in the Netherlands "general credit banks", and in other countries are often called commercial or deposit banks. The reason is that much the greater part of such banks, liabilities to their depositors perform the function of money in payment transactions, and that pro tanto the lending by these banks creates purchasing power. Such creation of purchasing power is however determined not by *the nature of the credit* which the banks grant, but by *the nature of the counterbalancing deposits and other possible liabilities*. If therefore one considers the monetary aspects of credit in a particular form (in this case at medium term), that makes sense only if and in so far as one thinks not of the lendings as such but of the possibility that the liabilities standing against them may be of a specific character. In other words, is any given expansion of medium-term lending accompanied by attraction of savings in the limited sense which I have just indicated? If so, then that part of the banks' business amounts to transmitting credit and not to creating purchasing power. Here therefore there would be no reason for measures to restrict credit, even on the assumption that general inflationary tendencies were prevailing.

This way of stating the problem implies recognition of the fact that the contrast drawn between lending out of savings and out of liquidity creation serves to typify ideas, and need not necessarily apply to particular groups of institutions which exist in real life. The ultimate criterion lies in the nature of the balance between loan and deposit accounts; since medium term credits are by definition of a lasting character, for these items the emphasis falls entirely on the liabilities standing against them.

To state the problem thus, however, makes it necessary to extend the analysis to all types of credit transmitting institutions. Just as it is not a priori clear that an ordinary bank by expanding its credits definitely *creates* purchasing power, so it is conceivable that other groups of credit institutions may be regarded as not solely *transmitting* credit. It may be true that particular types of credit institutions in general belong more to the one category than to the other; but this does not alter the fact that in the first place the dividing line may be variously drawn in different countries, and in the second place that certain institutions within these categories may have a twofold character.

Let us take just a few examples. In some countries saving banks must be regarded rather as creating purchasing power than as transmitting credit, although in others the opposite is regarded as obvious. What basically matters is how the account-holders behave, as a body, in connection with the relevant accounts. No clear answer to that question is given by the legal limitations to which the accounts are subject. Within those limitations, which of course in themselves are not without importance, the actual behaviour of the account-holders is what matters.

On the other hand there are credit institutions, such as (in the case of the Netherlands) the agricultural credit banks, the business of which can be functionally divided into a purchasing power creating and a credit-transmitting party. Prima facie this splitting can be based on the relation between demand and time deposits on the one hand, and savings accounts on the other; but essentially it is determined by the difference in behaviour of the various groups of depositors.

How then do matters stand in that respect in the case of the commercial banks? Is there evidence, in their case too, of any difference in behaviour as between various groups of their creditors?

During the last two years the commercial banks in the Netherlands have begun on a considerable scale to open savings accounts which, in one form or another, show a strong analogy with those of the savings banks, the agricultural credit banks and the Postal Savings Bank. If then at the same time increasing interest were to be shown in the granting of medium-term credit, would it not be logical to regard this whole section of the ordinary banks' business as monetarily irrelevant, and therefore to exclude it from any eventual restrictive measure designed to maintain monetary equilibrium? In dealing with this question I must begin by repeating that, while the legal relationships may perhaps afford a first indication, from the economic point of view they do not decide the matter.

Let us nevertheless look first at the legal relationships. It must at once be pointed out that within the general limitations to which "savings accounts" are subject, various special facilities are as a rule allowed in connection with them and these conflict with the character of a savings account in the functional meaning of that term as used by me. This applies for instance to the facilities granted in many cases for the making of payments in respect of transactions of certain kinds which are in themselves of a current nature – such as paying taxes and paying for public services like the telephone, gas and water. The same also applies however to payments which, regarded in themselves, do represent only a change in the form in which the property of the depositor is held. I mention, in this context, the purchase of securities out of savings-accounts. Such transactions, however, deprive the savings account of a part of its permanent character and make it into a kind of transit account. It applies a fortiori so far as the banks are prepared in practice to do away with the restrictions on withdrawals, either by permitting these before the due date against a discount on the agreed interest or by opening advance accounts against the deposit accounts.

What is however more important is, as already stated, the actual behaviour of the depositors. Even the most stringent restrictions as regards the right to draw on savings accounts leave open the possibility of calling balances on them at periods which are at variance with the lasting character of the credits granted against them. From the point of view of running its business this may entail not too much danger for the banking system as a whole, in so far as the liquidating of such accounts leads merely to an increase of its current account liabilities.

Since a large and fairly constant part of payment transactions is effected through settlement within the banking system, a switching of balances from savings to current accounts will reduce the individual bank's credit potential only in a limited degree. And, as soon as the process becomes general, it will a fortiori diminish only in limited measure the lending capacity of the banking system as a whole. There may even be no such diminution at all, if there is in general a growing tendency towards an increase of transfers in account by comparison with note and coin transactions. This tendency, which especially in a country like the Netherlands is clearly demonstrable, will above all occur during a period of economic expansion, when an increase of the country's total real capital resources expands payments, nearly all of which are made through transfers in accounts.

Finally, account must be taken of the possibility to which I referred earlier, namely that holders of "savings accounts" may, when making their arrangements to invest, nevertheless look upon these fixed claims as potential liquidity, so far as the payments entailed by such investment need to be made only in the future. This possibility will arise especially in the case of "savings" accounts belonging to entrepreneurs, and within that group will arise especially in times of booming business conditions.

In view of all this the monetary authorities will rightly be reluctant, to abstain from applying to those banks the observance of general restrictive regulations even in sofar as there is a more or less proportionate expansion of certain forms of long-term credits on the one hand and a growth of so-called savings accounts on the other hand.

Against this it has been urged that there is no need for such hesitation if the behaviour of holders of these savings accounts – which for the sake of convenience I shall from now on call "new" savings accounts – proves to be similar to that of the holders of what, also for the sake of convenience, I shall call the "traditional" savings accounts: that is, savings accounts with the typical credit-transmitting institutions. Whether it does prove to be similar could be deduced from comparison between the rates of turnover on both kinds of account.

In the Netherlands the average period during which balances are held on "traditional" savings accounts is 2 years at the savings banks, about 2½ years on savings accounts at the agricultural credit banks, and nearly 3½ years at the Postal Savings Bank. According to a calculation by one of the large banks the frequency of turnover on the "new" savings accounts held by it seems to be about 2 years. In the light of these figures one might say that both kinds of savings account are roughly of the same character. But the "traditional" savings accounts, and the long-term investments held against them, are excluded from credit control measures whereas these of the commercial banks are not. There might therefore seem to be some reason – when restrictive measures aiming at maintaining monetary equilibrium are applied to the commercial banks – to exclude from them the long-term lendings which stand against "savings" accounts, just as is done for instance in the case of the agricultural credit institutions.

That however would take no account of the relatively rapid growth of the "new" as compared with the "traditional" savings accounts. The "new" ones in fact show a proportionate rate of growth much faster than the "traditional" ones do. To that extent the figures for the *average* rate of turnover make balances on accounts of the former kind appear to stay there for longer than they really do. The point is that when the average frequency of turnover is calculated the first and the last in-payments are treated alike, regardless of the fact that withdrawals out of the monies first paid in are of course greater than those from the latest deposits. The more the real amount of the later in-payments exceeds that of the earlier ones, therefore, the less it will be possible to regard the significance of the average turnover rate as representative. Only when the rate of increase on the "new" savings accounts conforms to that on the "traditional" accounts does this objection lose its force. It will not disappear completely until the rates of increase on the "new" and "traditional" accounts have been equal for as long as balances on the first kind are on the average normally held.

Apart from a comparison between the average frequencies of turnover on the two kinds of accounts a comparison between the average size of balances on each might perhaps afford a pointer to the probable behaviour of account-holders. This average size is considerably greater on the "new" than on the "traditional" saving accounts. The bigger the balances are, the more likely they are either to have come from sale of capital assetsce anmelong to enterprises. So far as the former is the case, allow or to bust be made for the possibility that such accounts represent no really lasting form of investment, but serve in some measure as a transitional stage.

To dwell for a moment on the situation in the Netherlands, it must be observed that during recent years large amounts of Netherlands securities have constantly been sold to foreign countries, and that in many cases the proceeds of sale are left for some time awaiting a favourable moment for reinvestment. The fact that according to statements by the banks only a very small part of the balances on the "new" savings accounts are proceeds of securities sold abroad is irrelevant. It is quite conceivable that proceeds ofsecurity sales may be credited in the first place to a current account, and find their way only afterwards to savings accounts, which in their turn must be regarded as a more or less temporary investment.

Finally, as regards enterprises' accounts I can only repeat what I said before, namely that when investment is growing (and a fortiori when it is accompanied by a decrease of the cash flow) there will be a growing propensity to reckon the possibilities of drawing on "savings accounts" as claims which, while they cannot actually be regarded as liquid assets, can be converted into money whenever the acts of investment (which in themselves tend to stimulate economic activity) require the making of payments. Especially in the case of accounts that are kept not at specific savings institutions (with which the entrepreneur as a rule has no contact) but at the bank where the entrepreneur has his current account, the psychological forces tending to slow down such a process will be small.

In this connection let me say a brief word about inflationary effects which may possibly result from any new special institutions that are set up for the granting of medium-term credit, and which show a certain analogy with the phenomena I have just been talking about. In many cases, although medium-term credits will have to be promised at a given moment, the drawings on them will take place only gradually. The credit institution will then be faced with a difficult choice. Is it to take steps to ensure that it shall be able to dispose of the whole promised amount at once? Or shall it take such steps only at the time the drawings on the credits take place? In the former case it will lose interest, if the whole of the funds in question have to be at once procured in the capital market. In the latter the real effect is to anticipate savings which have not yet been formed. The first course is unattractive on business grounds; and that is just why there is an incentive to adopt the second. In the past we have seen examples of this. The second course produces a definitely inflationary effect, because the orders placed by the borrowers are already stimulating business activity at a time when the results of borrowing in the capital market are not yet tending to slow it down.

The conclusions to which all this leads appear to me to be as follows:

(1) The monetary authorities' supervision should not in principle be confined to lending (and a fortiori should not be confined to medium-term lending) out of current-account monies. It should also apply to medium-term lending out of deposits of third parties who may regard such deposits as having a fairly high degree of liquidity. The question whether there is reason to lay down general rules either about the expansion of credit as such, or about liquidity ratios, can be answered only in the light of facts which may vary from one country to another and from time to time. What matters is the extent to which the holders of these more or less tied accounts in fact continue or begin to regard balances on them as liquid.

(2) In general one can say that there will be more reason to apply equal treatment to medium-term credits granted respectively out of balances on savings accounts, time deposits and current accounts if there is a clear tendency for the banks to lengthen the periods of the loans granted by them, and if that process takes place in a time that is already beginning to show signs of over-expansion. This conclusion also applies to new medium-term credit institutions whose financing methods are still uncertain. In my view it even applies to "traditional" institutions, where these begin increasingly to open up possibilities to effect current payments out of "saving" accounts.

So far I have assumed throughout that there is in fact good reason for a relative expansion of medium-term credit. Before concluding these remarks, however, let me say a word or two about that assumption.

In making it I chiefly had in mind the situation in the Netherlands, which within a relatively short space of time has to a large extent grown from a trading into an industrial country, and which moreover faces the need to export a steadily increasing part of its national product. I also bore in mind that this trend has been accompanied in only limited measure by any structural change of the banking system, which is still mainly geared to the task of providing seasonal and commercial credits. The increasing capital requirements of the Netherlands' industries have been to a large extent met through retention of profits and through enlargement of their capital resources.

Regarded in itself, monetary stability will only be furthered by such method of financing. There comes however a point where it begins to do harm, insofar as it lures entrepreneurs into investments on which the marginal return drops too low and insofar as it places medium and small seized firms at a disadvantage as compared with the large and monopolistic ones. Finally a fall in profits – by no means an imaginary contingency – might prevent the continuing of fresh investment when this was prima facie desirable. In such circumstances the rapid advance of industrial techniques, and the consequent shortening of the economic life of various capital goods, may from the point of view of business management provide reasons for no longer finding the required funds entirely out of companies' own resources but for doing so by raising medium-term loans. Lengthening of the periods during which foreign customers have to be financed brings the industrialist into a field, increasingly outside his purview, where financial institutions are more at home. All this makes it understandable that, among industries, the interest shown in medium-term credits is growing. From the banking point of view moreover the potential liquidity of banks in the Netherlands is still particularly high, certainly as compared with that in other countries. In these circumstances a certain expansion of medium-term lending does in fact appear to be justified.

What applies to one country, however, does not necessarily apply to another. For that reason my assumption certainly claims no general validity.

But apart from de facto situations it can be said that, so far as *industry* is concerned, medium-term credits have a tendency to weaken its financial structure. At least they do this in so far as they are not used to repay immediately callable credits in current account, or some other from of short-term financing, but take the place of the companies' own capital resources inasmuch as they increase more quickly than these latter.

As regards the *banks*, even apart from the liquidity problems already discussed, any relative growth of medium-term lending must always entail additional risks by comparison with immediately callable loans. An increase of long-term lendings means that the banks pro tanto lose the power of intervening in good time, in the management of their debtors' affairs.

Any relatively large increase in the amount of medium-term credit will therefore tend to weaken the country's overall financial structure.

I must repeat, however, that a general statement like this is not intended to mean that such a development would be open to objection in all circumstances. As against this it may create opportunities for speeding up the general development process which fully justify such a course. Besides one should not forget that the improved understanding of monetary problems as a whole has considerably diminished the risk that individual insolvencies may create chain reactions. Still, the statement that a relatively rapid expansion of long or medium-term credit at least *tends* to weaken the solvency of a country's financial structure holds good. It does imply that, alongside the typically *monetary* aspects which have already been discussed and which are bound up with liquiity problems, the risk-factor may also assume monetary aspects. A bankruptcy may force the monetary authorities into a dilemma in which creation of liquidity, while in itself undesirable, may be the lesser of two evils. Where banks become involved in difficulties, even though on monetary grounds their financing policy cannot be called unduly inflationary, there is a danger that deposit money will be converted on a greater or lesser scale into notes and coin; and so the central bank, as lender of last resort, will have to decide on action in order to prevent general disturbance of equilibrium. Quite apart from the fact that the central bank thus assumes risks which the private sector (wrongly) supposed it safe to accept, it thereby loses its grip on the currency inasmuch as the holders of notes and coin are subject to no limitation on spending.

Even if one is prepared to admit that a large part of the money supply is tied by the transaction motive, to use a Keynesian term, regardless of the form in which it is held, there still remains the danger that mass conversion of savings balances into notes and coin may endanger monetary equilibrium. Not only from the banking point of view, but also on considerations of monetary policy, it is important that the solvency of the banking system shall remain unimpaired.

Finally one further remark. The industrial entrepreneur will strive for an optimum mean between the safeguards which his own capital and reserves will grant him, when conducting his business and the financial advantages of using money borrowed from third parties. In many instances it is taxation policy which causes this optimum mean, in the case of the individual entrepreneur, to be located at a point which is not justified from the point of view of the country's economy. For part of his business he may deem financing by credit profitable. Given the individual frequencies of turnover of particular stocks of goods, machinery and debtors he might even think it appropriate. This, however, is not so if the total amount of these items forms part of his permanent financial requirements. Financing through credit of permanent – although individually revolving items – while perhaps offering certain financial advantages to the entrepreneur, entails danger both for the borrower and for the lender.

It is dangerous for the borrower inasmuch as the transitional character of the machinery, stocks and debtors taken apart does not do away with the fact that financially they have to be considered as a lasting entity.

It is dangerous for the lender, inasmuch as he thereby becomes in reality a partner in an enterprise over which he can nevertheless exercise no more than very indirect supervision.

All this leads to the conclusion that for the monetary authorities, not only in view of the direct monetary aspects but also because of possible indirect consequences, there is every reason to devote special attention to medium-term bank credit. Not only have they to decide whether or not certain general rules as to liquidity should be declared to apply to it; they are also forced, in forming their policy, to pay due regard to the need for solidity in the whole financial structure of the country, and more particularly in that of its banking system.

Medium Term Credits in the United States of America

By William G. F. Price
Vice President, The Chase Manhattan Bank

You have asked me to talk with you on the subject of medium term credits in the United States of America. Throughout this paper it should be noted that any opinions expressed are solely those of the author. They do not necessarily represent the point of view of the institution with which the author is privileged to be identified.

So that we may follow the discussion together, I propose to divide the material into the following six subheadings:

First: We will define our terms.

Second: We will trace briefly the historical development.

Third: We will discuss some of the techniques involved in setting up medium term credits.

Fourth: The more important competitive sources of medium term credits will be explored.

Fifth: Certain questions of banking policy in this area will be examined.

Sixth: Some opinions with respect to future developments will be hazarded.

Definitions

How is medium term or intermediate credit defined? In the first place, intermediate credits are more commonly referred to in American usage as "term" loans. The most simple definition of a term loan is one which, by written agreement, has a final maturity beyond one year from the date on which the loan is made. While such a definition is correct, it fails to describe the characteristics which are inherent in most medium term credits. One authority describes a term loan as follows:

"A term loan generally has the following characteristics:

(1) The credit is advanced for a period of a minimum of one year with a maximum ordinarily of approximately ten years.

(2) Repayments are usually made serially over the life of the loan.

(3) Repayments are ordinarily made out of future earnings.

(4) The loan will customarily be accompanied by written covenants of the borrower to conduct his financial activities in a manner agreed upon by the borrower and the lender.

(5) The loan is usually made with a commercial bank, savings bank, insurance company, or a Government Lending Agency rather than sold by investment bankers to the public."[1]

To summarize, the essential elements usually found in a term loan transaction are:

(1) Maturities of one to ten years.

(2) Serial rather than a lump sum repayment.

(3) Future earnings are relied on for repayment.

(4) There is a written loan agreement which sets certain financial bench marks agreed upon by lender and borrower.

(5) The loan is privately placed with an institutional lender and not offered for public subscription.

The purposes for which the proceeds of term loans are employed, the types of business firms which use this facility, and the various American financial institutions which make intermediate credit available will be looked into subsequently in this discussion.

There are three other species of intermediate credit which are found in the portfolios of American commercial banks, i.e., consumer instalment loans, straight mortgage loans (as distinct from a term loan where a mortgage is at times taken as collateral security), and the bonds or debentures issued by industrial concerns, utilities, railroads, and local, state or the Federal Govern-

[1] Herbert V. Prochnow, *Term Loans and Theories of Bank Liquidity* (New York: Prentice Hall, 1949), p. 22.

ment or agencies thereof. Intermediate credits in the foregoing categories are excluded from our consideration. Each of these is a subject to itself. While it is readily recognized that credit extended in these categories is helpful to business, either directly or indirectly, it is our purpose to explore, in the main, this morning term loans, as defined, made by American commercial banks directly to business concerns.

Historical developments

Term loans, as we now know them, came on the American banking scene about 1933. However, it would be erroneous to conclude that prior to this date, American banks had not extended intermediate credit to business organizations. The explanation of this apparent paradox lies in the fact that, at least in its formative years, the American banking system adhered in form to the so-called "classical concept" of commercial banking, patterned after our British forbears; but both the structure of the American banking system as it developed, and the rapid growth of the country encouraged departure from that theory in practice.

The classical theory has been described as follows: "Briefly, this theory held that bank credit to business should take the form of short term advances to finance the production, storage or movement of goods, the ultimate sale of which would provide funds for liquidating the loans."[1]

Three specific references should suffice to make the point. Jacoby and Saulnier assert that at about the turn of the century, the amount of short term credit extended by American commercial banks to business was probably five times greater than the amount of long term credit granted.[2]

By 1913 "according to reports made to the Comptroller of the Currency[3] about 57% of all bank loans ... were made with original maturities of less than 90 days ... In 1940 ... about one-third of the commercial and industrial loans of all commercial banks

[1] Neil H. Jacoby and Raymond J. Soulnier, *Business Finance and Banking* (New York: National Bureau of Economic Research, 1947), p.132.

[2] *Business Finance and Banking*, p.135.

[3] The Comptroller of the Currency in the Unidet States is the Federal official charged with the responsibility of supervising the Federally chartered commercial banks. Such banks are known as National banks. Those institutions whose charters are granted by the various states are known as State banks.

consisted of term loans, with original maturities *exceeding* (the italics are the author's) one year ... Loans with maturities of 90 days or under can be estimated as comprising only slightly more than 30 percent of all business loans in 1940 as contrasted with 57% in 1913."[1]

Before citing our next quotation, two peculiarities of American banking practice should be made clear. With the exception of spaced maturities provided for in term loan agreements, the original maturity of a note all too frequently has no relationship to the date on which the debt created will be liquidated. One reason for this is the common practice of renewing notes at maturity when such action accords with the bankers' judgment and suits the borrower's convenience. Some evidence of the extent of this practice is afforded by two surveys. One was made of business loans made by banks which are members of the Federal Reserve System,[2] for a period beginning April 16 and ending May 15, 1942. Some 41% of the total loan volume for this period was accounted for by renewals of old loans. From the evidence it was concluded "that the majority of loans were renewed in whole or in part at their average maturity of 90 days."[3]

More recently – in October of 1955 – the Federal Reserve Bank of Cleveland made a survey of the business loans of the member banks in its district. This study "indicated that 61% of the dollar amount of the loans contained in the survey was continuous with the banks for one year or more; 38% of the dollar amount was continuous for three years or more, and 25% was continuous for 5 years or more."[4]

So much for the practice of renewing notes at maturity when the circumstances warrant.

The other American banking technique which accomplishes the result of keeping business loans short term in form, though not necessarily in fact, is known as "rotation," or shifting. In certain areas of my country the use of this device is not uncommon. When this practice is followed, it results in a periodic rotation

[1] *Business Finance and Banking*, p. 101.
[2] So-called member banks owned approximately 84% of the commercial bank assets of the country as of Dec. 30, 1959. *Federal Reserve Bulletin*, February 1960, p.173.
[3] *Business Finance and Banking*, p. 48.
[4] *Business Loans of American Commercial Banks*. Edited by B. Haggott Beckhart (New York City: Ronald Press, 1959), p. 148.

or shifting of a loan from one bank to another. This method of effecting payment of one bank's loans – usually for a month or so in a twelve month's period – by shifting the debt, in whole or in part, to another bank, pays homage to the classical theory of commercial banking by showing a payment of the loan on the books of any one bank even though this process negates the classical concept in substance. The facility with which borrowers can shift their debt from one bank to another has undoubtedly been enhanced by the development of the structure of the American banking system.

Had we followed the pattern of the British banking system, as in fact we attempted to do, it would probably have resulted in our country having relatively few banks, each having a large number of branches located across the country. Instead, largely for political reasons, we did develop a so-called "independent" banking system. The political considerations had to do with the broad question of state versus federal control. They were also concerned with the fact that as our country developed geographically the growth was from East to West. Hence there was an understandable mistrust of permitting too great a concentration of economic and financial power along the Eastern seaboard.

Thus our banking system is featured by a very large number of institutions, the stock ownership of each being independent of any other. At the peak, in 1921, there were almost 30,000 commercial banks in the United States.[1] Since that time the tendency has been for the number of banks to decrease. This has been due to a variety of reasons which are beyond the purview of this paper. Suffice it to say that as of today, the number of commercial banks in our country is approximately 13,500.[2] With this relatively large number of banks available, it is not at all uncommon for a concern of comparatively modest size to have two or more banks. Moreover, it is not unusual in certain localities to have such companies shift their bank borrowings from one bank to another without at any one time effecting complete liquidation of bank debt in toto. So far as it is known here, there are no statistics available to measure the volume of bank debt that is so shifted.

[1] *Banking and Monetary Statistics* (Washington, D. C.: Board of Governors, Federal Reserve System, 1943), p.19.

[2] *Federal Reserve Bulletin*, February 1960, p.173.

However, it is clearly of sufficient magnitude to have developed a second theory of bank liquidity known as shiftability in addition to the classical theory of truly self-liquidating loans. This principle of shiftability has been described as follows: "As banks digressed from this principle (i.e., self-liquidating loans) and made loans that were not self-liquidating, they often relied on transfer of the loan to another lender, or on the sale of collateral. This has been called the 'shiftability theory.' This theory did not work very well in a period of economic depression. If prices of collateral declined or other banks or lenders withdrew from the market at the same time, there was 'no place to shift to' and no market for sale. The shiftability theory did not work in 1929-33."[1] [2] As will be pointed out later, the "shiftability" of bank assets to the central banks, as distinct from bank to bank, (in the case of the United States the 12 Federal Reserve Banks) is the ultimate source of liquidity of the commercial banking system.

Underlying these two stratagems (renewal of short term paper and rotation of debt between banks) for adhering *in form* to the classical theory of commercial bank lending, there was undoubtedly a basic economic need. That was the necessity for capital loans by business in a young country, fortunately rich in natural resources, with a seemingly boundless frontier, with an expanding population, and with a shortage of capital. Partly because that need still exists (perhaps for somewhat different reasons) and partly because these two devices have become so firmly imbedded in American banking practice, it is doubtful whether either practice will be discarded in the foreseeable future.

In summary, then, it may be said that while loans which were long term by agreement, other than mortgage loans, were frowned upon by American commercial banks prior to 1933, in fact such long term loans were made. In deference to the classical theory of commercial banking, most notes were made short term in tenor. At maturity many notes were either renewed or shifted to another bank. The basic reason was a need for long term loans in a country which was confronted with a shortage of capital.

[1] *Business Loans of American Commercial Banks*, p. 256.

[2] For a further discussion of shiftability see *Term Loans and Theories of Bank Liquidity* and *Business Loans of American Commercial Banks*, pp. 22–25.

Developments circa 1933

It is interesting to inquire into the reasons which motivated the American commercial banks beginning about 1933 to take a new look at the requirements of American business for capital loans. Sometimes much loans are referred to as medium term or intermediate credits, sometimes as term loans.

At this point one is reminded of a quotation from that most quotable of all English authors – Shakespeare:

"*There is a tide in the affairs of men which, taken at the flood, leads on to fortune;*
Omitted, all the voyage of their life is bound in shallows and in miseries."

1933 was such a time in the "tide" of the American commercial banks. The tide was at the flood, if liquidity were the criterion, at the ebb from an earnings point of view. Here in figures was the picture with respect to all member banks as of Dec. 30, 1933:[1]

Total deposits	$27.2 billion
Total loans	$12.8 billion

In other words, loans represented about 47% of deposits.

Investments stood at $12.4 billion, about the same amount as loans, but of these investments about 60% consisted of U.S. Government securities, cash items amounted to about $6.5 billion. If one took off a 100% balance sheet (total assets equal 100%) of the American commercial banking system – as exemplified by all member banks as of December 30, 1933, the following picture would be revealed.[1*]

Thus we had a banking system with better than 55% of its total resources in Cash and Securities, less than 40% invested in loans, and somewhat more than 15% in those classified as business loans. Loans were substantially less than three times capital funds and were appreciably less than 50% of deposits. Business loans per se were about 20% of deposits.

This preference for liquidity is easily understood when it is realized that deposits which had reached their peak of $39 billion on December 31, 1928 had declined in five years to $27 billion, a drop of close to 33⅓%. The banking system up to this point had little choice but to get liquid and stay that way.

[1] *Banking and Monetary Statistics*, pp.74 – 77.
* *Tabel 1 p. 95*

TABLE 1
Assets

Cash and Cash Items		19.1%
U.S. Government Securities	21.4%	
Other Securities	15.2%	
Total Securities		36.6%
Loans on Securities	14.5%	
Real Estate Loans	7.0%	
Other Loans – largely commercial, industrial and agricultural	16.5%	
Total Loans		38.0%
Bank Premises		2.9%
Customers Liability on Acceptances		1.4%
Other Assets		2.0%
TOTAL ASSETS		100.0%

Liabilities

Demand Deposits	55.9%	
Time Deposits	24.4%	
Total Deposits		80.3%
Borrowings		.5%
Acceptances		1.5%
Other Liabilities		3.1%
Capital Accounts		14.8%
TOTAL LIABILITIES PLUS CAPITAL		100.0%

Totals will not necessarily prove because of rounding.

When earnings at that time were examined, as one might expect, the picture was painted in drab tones. The prevailing rate on prime commercial paper had reached a peak of $6\frac{1}{4}$% in September–October of 1929. This had fallen, in an almost uninterrupted decline, to $1\frac{3}{8}$% by the end of 1933. It was to go still lower before the turn came some seven years later. The rate on call loans on the New York Stock Exchange had gone to 14% in the forepart of 1929. This had plummeted to 1% or less by the end of 1933.[1]

The average yield on 3–6 month U.S. Government paper had reached a high point of 4.7% in October of 1928. By the end of 1933 it was .25% and at times during the year it had been as low as .01%.[2] Bond yields did not follow the general downward trend in rates, presumably because of the almost constant pressure for liquidation. Triple A bonds were selling to yield 4.8% in September of 1929. At this time U.S. Government bonds were quoted on a 3.7% basis. In December of 1933 Triple A's were selling at a 4.5% return and long term Governments had dropped only to 3.5%.[3] As it will be pointed out later, the wide spread between bank interest rates and bond yields was one important inducement for corporate financial officers to refund outstanding public issues with long term bank loans.

This severe drop in interest rates in the short term sector combined with the shrinkage in resources, already referred to, was of course reflected in the banks' earning figures. By way of contrast here are two earnings statements for all member banks, one for the year 1929 and the other for 1933:[4]

TABLE 2

	1929	1933
Interest and Discount on Loans	65.2%	48.8%
Interest and Dividends on Securities	19.7	34.5
Other Current Earnings	15.1	16.7
TOTAL EARNINGS	100.0%	100.0%
Salaries and Wages	19.3%	24.8%
Interest on Deposits	31.7	23.3
Other Current Expenses	19.2	21.4
TOTAL EXPENSES	70.2%	69.5%
NET CURRENT EARNINGS	29.8%	30.5%

[1] *Banking and Monetary Statistics*, pp.450 – 451, 456 – 457.
[2] *Banking and Monetary Statistics*, p.460.
[3] *Ibid.*, pp.469 – 470.
Ibid., pp.264 – 265.

Thus it will be seen that in four short years interest and discount on loans dropped from producing about two-thirds of total income to account for less than half. This decline was a function of shrinking volume and the collapse of short term interest rates. The same two factors account for the drop in the percentage of total income applied to interest on deposits. The increase in Salaries and Wages is, of course, relative, not absolute. While in both years approximately 30% of gross income was carried through to net, there were dramatic shifts in the composition of both income and expense. Before leaving this phase of our look at earnings, two sets of absolute figures should be mentioned.[1]

TABLE 3

ALL MEMBER BANKS
(000 Omitted)

	1929	1933	% + or –
Gross Earnings	$2,398,993	$1,236,864	– 48.4%
Expenses	1,683,720	859,300	– 48.9
Net Current Earnings	715,273	377,564	– 47.1
Recoveries on Loans and Securities and Profit on Securities Sold	136,714	124,885	– 8.2
	851,987	502,449	– 41,1%
Losses and Depreciation on Loans and Securities and on Banking Houses and Equipment	295,473	858,279	+197.3%
Net Profits	556,514	– 355,830	

These figures make clear the extent of the effects of the Great Depression on the American commercial banking system. Both Gross Earnings and Net Current Earnings were virtually cut in half. In the four year period the final figure of Net Profits, i.e.,

[1] *Ibid.*, pp. 262 – 263.

Net Current Earnings plus recoveries and minus losses, had swung from a black figure of $556 million to a red one of $356 million, a shift of over $900 million. Incidentally, the net profit figure for 1932 was minus $255 million and minus $245 million for 1934. In those three years alone the net profits of all member banks was written in red ink to the tune of $856 million.

To complete our review of the earnings situation one further brief look at some figures is desirable:

TABLE 4

	All Member Banks		
	1929	1933	% + or –
Ratios to Total Capital Accounts			
Net Current Earnings	11.2	7.2	– 36.3
Net Charge-offs	2.4	11.7	+ 385.8
Net Profits	8.8	–4.5	
Ratios to Total Assets			
Total Earnings	5.1	3.7	– 26.7
Total Expenses	3.6	2.6	– 27.8
Net Current Earnings	1.5	1.1	– 26.7
Net Charge-offs	.3	2.2	+ 633.3
Net Profits	1.2	–1.1	
Ratios to Loans			
Interest and Discount on Loans	6.1	4.7	– 23.0
Recoveries on Loans	.1	.2	+ 100.0
Losses on Loans	.5	3.3	+ 560.0
Net Return on Loans	5.7	1.6	– 71.9
Ratios to Securities			
Interest and Dividends on Securities	4.7	3.5	– 25.5
Recoveries on Securities	.2 }	.7	– 22.2
Profits on Securities Sold	.7 }		
Losses on Securities	.9	2.9	+ 222.2
Net Return on Securities	4.7	1.3	– 72.3

[1] *Ibid.*, pp.264 – 265.

A review of the figures connected with bank earnings makes it very clear that regardless of the standard of measurement used, the inroads made on the earning capacity of the American commercial banking system were severe. In addition to the shift in the composition of the earning assets from loans to securities, there was a drop in the dollar amount of net current earnings of close to 50%. Reflected in these figures, of course, is the collapse in short term rates which was referred to previously.

On a net profit basis between 1929 and 1933, the change was to a substantial red figure which amounted to nearly two-thirds of the impressive black figure reported for 1929. As a result of these changes, net current earnings on banking capital dropped from about 11% to around 7%. As measured by return on total assets, the decline was from 1½% to a shade over 1%. The deterioration took place in both major classes of earning assets. Gross return on loans (before Recoveries and Losses) went from a little better than 6% to about 4¾%. On a net basis (after Recoveries and Losses) the slippage was even more drastic, going down from about 5¾% to a little bit above 1½%.

"The fate of the return on securities was parallel. On a gross basis the yield was reduced from about 4¾% to around 3½%. After giving effect to Recoveries and Profits and Losses, the figure moved from about 4¾% to a little bit above 1¼%."

The analysis of the banking figures for 1933 warrants two conclusions. The first is that from a liquidity point of view the banking system could well afford to flex its muscles with respect to increasing its loan volume, as well as to exploring new fields of lending. The second inference, from the income angle, made it apparent that such a course of action would be highly desirable if not imperative.

So much for the banking supply side. Now for a brief glance at the business demand side.

To quantify the business demand side of the equation as it existed in 1933 poses a much more difficult problem. A few isolated statistics do, however, throw some light on the issue. The following is a schedule of actual gross property expenditures for all non-financial corporations for the years indicated:[1]

[1] *Regularization of Business Investment* (Princeton N. J: National Bureau of Economic Research; Princeton University Press, 1954), p.403.

1929		$10.3 billion
1930		4.5 billion
1931		1.1 billion
1932	—	0.3 billion
1933		3.4 billion

This compared with such expenditures for the three prior years to 1929 which ranged from $8.2 billion to $8.9 billion per annum. Outlays for new plant and equipment in 1929 were estimated to have exceeded $9 billion. This had dropped successively to about $2 billion in 1933.[1] Corporate profits, after taxes, in 1929 were close to $9 billion. In 1932 there was a net loss of some $6 billion. In 1933 American business hardly broke even.[2]

Investment in inventories is, along with fixed assets, another major source of business expenditures. In the year 1929 manufacturers' inventories were estimated to be close to $14 billion. In 1932 they had been cut back ot about $8 billion. During 1933 they had been rebuilt to the extent of some $1 billion. Manufacturers' sales in the same period had tobogganed from better than $70 billion in 1929 to around $31 billion in 1932 and then moved up by some $5 billion in 1933.[3]

One other indication as to the possible need by business for long term money is afforded by what happened with respect to the issue of corporate securities during 1929 to 1933. Corporate securities in 1929 were floated in an amount in excess of $7 billion, divided roughly 80% for new capital and 20% for refunding. In 1933 less than 400 million of corporate securities came on the market, about one-third being for new money and two-thirds for refunding. It is significant to note that in 1936, just three years later, about $4.6 billion of securities were offered. About 75% of these were for the purpose of raising new capital, 25% for refunding.[4] During these same years, business loans of the member banks increased from a little under $5 billion to a little over $6 billion.[5]

[1] *Historical Supplement to Federal Reserve Chart Book* (Washington, D. C.: Board of Governors, Federal Reserve System, September 1959).

[2] *Ibid.*, p. 64.

[3] Moses Abramovitz. *Inventories and Business Cycles* (New York City: National Bureau of Economic Research, 1950), p. 111.

[4] *Federal Reserve Chart Book*, p. 60.

[5] *Banking and Monetary Statistics*, p. 76.

Putting these random facts together, the following picture begins to emerge. The sales curve started its upward climb in 1933 after a steep descent beginning in 1929. During this period, business profits had gone from a plus to a minus figure and then struggled back to about a break-even basis. Business management had understandably severely cut back its expenditures for plant and equipment and inventories. Undoubtedly neither of these important business assets were in proper condition to adequately service even a moderate upswing in volume. Because of the prevailing economic climate, the oversold condition of the securities markets and the resistance of the long term interest rate, American corporations had indeed made sparing use of the public securities markets. The need for long term capital would seem to have been apparent even though the extent of the need might be difficult to gauge accurately. To have restored manufacturers' inventories to their 1929 level would have required $5 to $6 billion. If $8.5 billion per annum might be considered a pre-1929 level of expenditures for fixed assets, then an outlay of close to $17 billion would have been required to compensate for the ravages in this sector which took place from 1930 through 1933. One authority sums up the situation from the business man's point of view in the following words: "In the easy money period following the Great Depression, many companies sought to retire high rate bond issues sold in the 1920's to achieve interest savings, to reduce fixed charges, to simplify capital structures, to revise maturities to currently projected cash flow and needs, and to eliminate burdensome mortgage or indenture provisions. Since corporate bonds with the rating of AA averaged 4.82 per cent in 1928-29 and the prime bank rate was 1.50 per cent from 1934 to 1947, with term rates not substantially higher, this became a common practice for companies in good credit standing. ... As business recovered from the depression, increasingly larger funds were needed for deferred maintenance and for new machinery and plants able to meet new competitive conditions, to offset rising labor costs with labor-saving machinery, to decentralize production, and to provide regional manufacturing facilities, to offset rising freight rates. World War II brought enormous industrial expansion to meet business and defense needs. The rising population curves which followed World War II and the Korean War, with the accompanying expansion of credit and subsequent inflation of costs, produced cash requirements beyond internal cash generation and resulted in a demand for bank term credit as one source of needed funds."[1]

Developments since 1933

Before examining the extent of term loans, several broad developments should be mentioned which facilitated the growth of this type of loan. The first was the tremendous increase in excess reserves which started about 1933, caused in substantial part by the enormous influx of gold. Excess reserves at the end of 1933 amounted to $766 million. Our gold stock was approximately $2.7 billion. Free reserves hit the staggering peak of close to $7 billion in October of 1940 – an increase of over $6 billion. Our supply of gold had increased to over $21 billion in the same month, a growth of close to $19 billion.[2] This not only exerted a tremendous pressure on rates but was a powerful incentive for bankers to put these funds to work.

The second stimulating factor was the passage of The Securities Act of 1933 and the Securities Exchange Act of 1934. These Acts "placed some restrictions on business access to public investment markets. Business men and directors were fearful of the 'tough' liability provisions of the law; the delays of registration involved risks of not being financially covered; the prospectus involved competitive disclosures some business men did not want to make. These procedures raised the cost of public financing. ... Bank term loans could be negotiated quickly without these disadvantages."[3]

A third major cause of growth of term loans was a change in the attitude of the bank examiners in their classification of bank loans. Prior to 1934, loans, other than those which were passed without comment, were put into three criticized categories:

(a) Estimated Loss

(b) Doubtful

(c) Slow – i.e., generally, loans which had not been fully liquidated within a year of their expiration.

[1] *Business Loans of American Commercial Banks*, pp. 210–211.
[2] *Banking and Monetary Statistics*, pp. 371–372.
[3] *Business Loans of American Commercial Banks*, p. 210.

By and large bankers who had made so-called slow loans were under considerable pressure to effect their liquidation in the reasonably near future. In 1934 there was an "informal" relaxation with respect to so-called slow loans in those cases where the examiners were satisfied that ultimate repayment of the loan on a reducing basis seemed well assured. In 1938 the "slow" rating was eliminated and a new classification "Other Loans Especially Mentioned" was substituted. With respect to this rating, examiners tended to omit from their report those loans where the sole basis of criticism was failure to clear within one year.

Other broad developments favoring an increase in intermediate credits have been cited. They are listed as follows::

(1) The broadening rediscount and advance provisions of the Federal Reserve Banks to their members reduced the need for independent liquidity. These changes were authorized in the Banking Acts of 1933 and 1934.

(2) The inauguration of the Federal Deposit Insurance Corporation in 1933 had reduced the likelihood of Bank runs. These had been a plague during the depression.

(3) Authorization in June 1934 to the Federal Reserve Banks and the Reconstruction Finance Corporation not only to make term loans but to participate with commercial banks in term loans made by the latter.

(4) The introduction of the amortized mortgage by the Federal Housing Administration influenced commercial bank lending policies by placing more emphasis on income than on collateral security.

(5) Another change in the attitude of the examining authorities which had to do with valuing the bond account. Prior to 1938, if the cost of a bond exceeded the market value, such excess had to be written off as an "estimated loss." Based on the experience which banks had in the bond market 1929–1933, this ruling had a tendency to steer them out of the bond market and into term loans. Since 1938 highly rated bonds may be carried at cost less the amortiza-

tion of the premium, if any. Lower quality bonds may be valued at the average market price for the prior 18 months.[1]

While this reversal in 1938 with respect to the pricing of the bonds in a bank investment account would appear in theory to be a deterrent to term lending, in fact, the focus of bank thinking had been changed in the intervening years.

Volume of term loans

When it comes to measuring the extent of term loans in the American commercial banking system, one is confronted with a significant gap in banking statistics. Continuous data is not published with respect to term loans. Occasional surveys have been made by the Federal Reserve Board, as well as by other reputable organizations. There, however, have been at random dates. It is also felt here that there probably is some lack of uniformity as to the basis on which individual banks report their activity in this field. Despite these deficiencies in the available tools of measurement, the evidence seems to point conclusively to the fact that such intermediate credits have become significantly more important in the American banking and business scheme of things.

The first survey of term lending made by the Federal Reserve Board was undertaken as of April 19, 1939 and the results published in the Federal Reserve Bulletin – July 1939, pp. 560-562. This covered about 400 of the larger banks in 101 leading cities. These banks held approximately $4 billion of commercial, industrial and agricultural loans. This comprised about 70% of such loans outstanding with all member banks. Of this $4 billion of business loans, about 1 billion, or 25%, had an original maturity of one year or longer. There was also an additional total of about 175 million of intermediate loans to business houses secured by real estate, out of a total of 1 billion of real estate loans.

In 1941 the National Bureau of Economic Research conducted a thorough study of term lending. Their inquiry covered 99 large banks whose assets represented almost 50% of the assets of all member banks. From this information they compiled the schedule which follows:[2]

[1] *Term Lending to Business*, pp. 22–28.
[2] *Ibid.*, p. 76.

Outstanding December 31	Term Loans of 56 Reporting Banks (Actual) (a)	Term Loans of All Commercial Banks (Estimated)	Total Loans of All Commercial Banks (Actual)	Term Loans as a percentage of Total Loans
	(Figures are in millions)			
1935	215	No Estimate	15,164	–
1936	337	No Estimate	16,415	–
1937	370	827	17.190	4.8
1938	485	1,083	16,440	6.6
1939	714	1,596	17,263	9.2
1940	967	2,162	18,830	11.5

(a) of the 99 banks surveyed, 56 supplied year end figures of term loans outstanding going back to 1935.

From the estimated data of term loans of all commercial banks, the following table has been constructed:

Outstanding December 31	Term Loans of all CommercialBanks (Estimated)	Business Loans of all Member Banks (a)[1]	Term Loans of all Commercial Banks as a Percentage of Business Loans of all Member Banks
	(Figures in Millions)		
1937	827	6,996	11.8
1938	1,083	5,449	19.9
1939	1,596	6,116	26.1
1940	2,162	7,069	30.6

(a) Figures for 1937 – – not strictly comparable to 1938-1940 because of a change in loan classifications.

While the statistical validity of comparing Term Loans of *all* commercial banks with the Business Loans of all *member* banks is open to some doubt, it is believed that the relationship does have significance. It is certain that for this period term loans had not only grown substantially in dollar totals but as a percentage of both total loans and business loans as well.

The most recent surveys conducted by the Federal Reserve Board have been under dates of November 20, 1946, October 5, 1955, and October 16, 1957.[2]

[1] *Banking and Monetary Statistics*, p.76.

[2] *Federal Reserve Bulletins as* follows: Nov. 20, 1946 survey – May 1947, pp.498 – 517. Oct. 5, 1955 survey – April 1956, pp.327 – 40. Oct. 16, 1957 survey – April 1959, pp.353 – 68.

The following table has been developed, based on the three surveys just mentioned:

All Member Banks
(In Millions of Dollars)

Date	Term Loans	Total Business Loans	Percentage of Term Loans to Total Business Loans
Nov. 20, 1946	4,558	13,189	34.5
Oct. 5,1955	10,457	30,820	33.9
Oct. 17, 1957	15,421	40,582	38.0

In perspective, the growth of intermediate credit in the American commercial banking system has been explosive. The earliest estimate for *all commercial banks* made in 1937 arrived at a figure of about $800 million. The latest survey under date of October 1957 shows term loans outstanding for *all member banks* at over $15 billion. In terms of the percentage of total business loans, the sampling made by the Federal Reserve Board in 1939 indicates that loans with an original maturity of more than one year amounted to about 25%. The latest survey shows it to be 38% of aggregate business loans of all member banks. It is of interest to point out that this total (i.e. of business loans) had grown from around $5½ billion in 1938 to over $40 billion in 1957. It is also pertinent to note that total loans in this interval of time had increased from around $13 billion to around $80 billion. As a percentage of total loans, business loans had increased from 41% to 47%. More will be said about this phase of the matter when the discussion of policy is undertaken. It is sincerely to be hoped that banking figures on this important intermediate segment of the loan portfolio will be published on a regular and uniform basis.

Characteristics of borrowers and lenders

A few more highlights based on the 1957 survey will complete our consideration of historical background and growth. There is no such prototype as a "typical term loan borrower." The industries served cover the whole range of the American business scene from small service companies to the very large corporations which tend to be predominant in such industries as metals, petroleum and transportation. This group of heavy industries accounted for 40% of the dollars loaned, though only about 13% in number of loans.

When it comes to the size of the borrower, as measured by total assets, the spectrum is also broad, running from those companies th assets of less than $50 thousand to those with assets of $100 million and more. Those companies having assets of less than $250M had around 20% of the dollars but accounted for some 80% of the number of loans. Borrowers controlling assets of $5 million or more used about 50% of the funds. In number of loans they were responsible for above 2%.

As far as maturities are concerned, the average maturity date was in excess of 5 years. However, the trend since 1946 has been towards shortening maturities. From 1955 to 1957 the sharpest growth was in loans of one to three years. There were a relatively small number of loans with final maturities of more than ten years.

Interest rates on term loans are matters of negotiation, depending on the size of the loan, the term, the strength of the borrower, whether or not the loans are secured, and the type of security pledged. Generally the smaller loans are secured and the larger ones tend to be unsecured. There are of course exceptions to the rule. Loans to transportation companies and certain petroleum loans, for example, even though to large borrowers, might well be secured. The smaller loans for obvious reasons customarily carry higher rates. In the 1957 survey, effective rates ranged from 4.05% to 9.96%.[1]

In the 1957 survey no report was made with respect to secured vs. unsecured loans. Such information was gathered in the 1955 investigation. Of the total loans of $10.5 billion then outstanding, 41% in amount were unsecured and 59% were secured. For those borrowers with assets of less than $250M, some 94% were secured and 6% not. For the group owning resources of $5 million to $25 million, the proportions were about 50-50. For the very largest group (assets of $100 million and over), the ratio

[1] Effective rates above 6% are apt to apply to loans repayable in monthly installments where the interest is added on to the amount the borrower wishes to realize and then this total amount is discounted.

was 77% unsecured and 23% secured. The three most important types of property pledged were:

Plant and Real Estate, which accounted for 38% of all secured loans;

Equipment, which accounted for 25% of all secured loans, and

Assignment of claims (such as Accounts Receivable, Moneys due or to become due under contracts), which accounted for 17% of all secured loans.

Two more figures are needed to fill out our picture. The first has to do with the size distribution of the banks making term loans. Based on the 1957 survey, here is the story on this point:

Size of Bank (Total Deposits in Millions)	% of Dollars of Term loans Held
less than 10	3.8
10 – 100	13.4
100 to 1,000	28.6
1000 and over	54.2
	100.0

On the last detail, i.e., the extent of participation by banks, other than the originating institution, the 1957 study was silent. The figures quoted are therefore based on the findings of 1955.

Total Term Loans	No participation Dollars	%	Participation Dollars	%
(all figures in millions)				
10,457	7,158	86.5	3,300	31.5

Participations arise for one of these three basic reasons:

the amount of the credit requested exceeds the legal capacity of the originating bank;

the originating bank, because of the size of the loan, may consider it prudent or desirable to share the risk; or

if the borrower is of a size which justifies the maintenance of two or more banks of deposit, he may desire that the loan be spread.

Since the latter two causes are more important than the first, it is natural to expect what the figures show: namely, a much greater degree of participation by the larger banks (43% for banks with over $1 billion in deposits as against 5% for those banks with less than $10 million). There is also a greater spreading of the risk in the longer maturities (50% for the larger banks with loans running over 5 years as against 33% with loans maturing within 5 years).

A review of the foregoing surveys, as well as the literature in the field leads to two conclusions. At the inception of term lending on a formalized basis, there was a tendency to have such credits in the main arranged by the larger banks, with the proceeds being made available to only the larger borrowers. However, as the demand grew and the techniques became better understood, the program diffused through the banking and business system. As matters now stand, intermediate credits are available to worthy borrowers in all size categories and even the smallest banks will entertain medium term credit applications. Terms and conditions regarding rate, maturity, and security are generally matters of individual negotiation.

Technique

Having completed the historical survey of intermediate credits, brief attention will now be given to the technique of appraising such credits and of setting up and following the loans.[1] No attempt will be made here to go into great detail. Rather it is the objective to state major principles:

One of the broad avenues which exist for the repayment of

[1] For those who are interested in a more detailed discussion of the practical aspects of making term loans than the scope of this paper will permit, reference is made to the following sources previously referred to:

Term Lending by Commercial Banks, 1945;
Business Finance and Banking, 1947;
Term Loans and Theories of Bank Liquidity, 1949;
Business Loans of American Commercial Banks, 1959, chapter 9.

Also several excellent theses on this subject have been submitted by experienced bankers as a partial requirement for graduation from the Graduate School of Banking. The latter is an adult educational enterprise conducted jointly by the American Bankers Association, 12 East 36th St., New York 16, N. Y. and Rutgers University, New Brunswick, New Jersey. Such theses are on file at the Library of the American Bankers Association, the Library at Rutgers University, and the Library of the Graduate School of Business at Harvard University, Cambridge, Massachusetts.

loans is the conversion of assets into cash in the normal operation of the business. (As inventories are processed and sold, they turn into receivables. As the latter are collected they flow into cash.) The second means of loan repayment is retained earnings. These at times are buttressed by depreciation which is not required to be spent immediately to replace the assets depreciated. It is obvious that the degree of risk in the latter class of loans tends to be greater than in the first group of advances. This is true for three reasons. The conversion of assets is usually accomplished on a short term seasonal basis. Moreover, the funds borrowed generally are directly reflected in working capital. Typically, the proceeds of term loans are more apt to go into fixed or capital assets. Lastly, since term loans involve an estimate of future developments over a period of years, they are subject to the manifold hazards which are necessarily involved in attempting to forecast what lies ahead.

Therefore, in addition to the analysis of balance sheets and earnings statements which bankers are accustomed to make when appraising any credit application, when it comes to term loans, a much more searching look must be given to a long historical review of past earnings and balance sheet trends. This is in the hope that at least such a perspective may give a clue as to what may be expected to occur down the road ahead.

Because history does have a habit at times of *not* repeating itself, it is a fairly common requirement for bankers to request a projection of cash income and expenditures (commonly known as a cash flow budget), where management is not already operating on such a basis for its own guidance. How far ahead such forecasts should attempt to cover (1 year, 5 years, or even longer) is a matter of judgement. For instance, a long range forecast of a well established public utility, with a long record of earnings and located in a diversified and growing community might be expected to have a higher degree of accuracy than a long range estimate of a manufacturer in the more volatile textile trades.

Fully as important as earnings, if not even more so, are certain intangible aspects. Not only must one be satisfied with the present management of an enterprise, but the question arises of a competent succession in the event that some untoward development might deprive the enterprise of the services of its current executives before the final maturity of the long term loan.

Competitive conditions within the industry must also be carefully appraised. With the great multiplicity of new products constantly reaching the market, competition with such items must also be taken into account. A fairly recent example of this is the still undetermined final effect of television on the motion picture industry. Applications for intermediate credits in lines of business which seem to be in a long range decline (men's hats might be an instance) must be reviewed with unusual care. At the other extreme, in certain relatively new and booming industries (electronics, for example), unless a strongly intrenched company is under consideration, it takes unusual perspicacity to differentiate between the relatively large number of newcomers in what promises to be a burgeoning industry.

Reverting to financial criteria, enough strength should be evident in the balance sheet and a sufficiently large margin of anticipated earnings over required payments projected to enable a company to weather a storm of reasonable length and severity. While it may be true, as some have asserted, that we will not be subjected to another "Great Depression," it certainly is clear that business cycles are not a phenomenon of the past. It would be disconcerting to put on a term loan that got into "trouble" within a year or two of its inception. Indeed, it is embarrassing enough to have obligated one's self to an intermediate credit which encounters difficulties during its lifetime. To take one on which encounters shoal water within the first several months of its existence is bound to raise questions in the mind of the grantor as to how well he appraised the situation originally.

The next step, after the banker has satisfied himself as to the credit worthiness of the borrower for the amount and the term involved, is to trade out the specific conditions governing the loan. Almost invariably term loans are made subject to the provisions of a written loan agreement. There is no set form for such a document. Each is tailor made to fit the individual circumstances. Some are quite simple in form, taking up no more than three or four written pages. Others become quite formidable, in both length and content.

Whether long or short, these written term loan agreements usually break down into five parts. The first contains certain warranties made by the borrower; the second includes specific requirements which the borrower agrees to meet, usually called affirmative covenants; the third refers to certain acts which the borrower binds himself not to perform or to events which the borrower agrees to prevent occurring. It is usually specified that if they should occur the borrower will correct the situation. These conditions are usually referred to as "negative covenants"; the fourth section details the rights of the lender in the event of the breach of any warranty or the occurrence of any default in any of the affirmative or negative covenants; and the last section generally deals with what constitutes legal notice under the agreement. There is also frequently a section dealing with prepayments and the penalties which the borrower may be called on to foot should he elect to prepay the loan in whole or in part. Specimen loan agreements are given in many of the sources mentioned in the beginning of this section. Since the intent of this portion of the paper is not to go into detail on technique and since the first and the fifth portions of a term loan agreement are essentially legal in character, any discussion of them here will be omitted. An effort will be made to discuss the highlights of the portions of the term loan agreement which deal with affirmative and negative covenants, rights in event of default, and prepayment provisions

The most important single affirmative covenant is the agreement on the part of management to maintain an agreed floor under working capital i.e. current assets less current liabilities. This, of course, applies to companies where adequate working capital is essential to a sound operation. It has but limited significance to companies whose sales are on a cash basis, where inventories are an insignificant percentage of total assets and whose success is primarily dependent on the maintenance and earning capacity of their fixed assets. In the latter category would be the service industries, including transportation. The same reasoning would apply to oil production loans where the source of repayment consists of proven oil reserves. By and large the maintenance of an agreed level of working capital is essential for a company engaged in the production and/or sale of goods on credit where the maintenance of balanced inventories is necessary for the proper conduct of the business.

The aim in determining the level of working capital is to set a figure which is not so high that it will unduly hamper management in the day by day conduct of the business. At the same time it should not be set so low that the affairs of the borrower can deteriorate to a dangerous level before the lender has an opportunity to "take another look." More will be said about this under events of default. Sometimes there are also included covenants with respect to the maintenance of a minimum current and/or quick ratio. The former has to do with the proportion of current assets to current liabilities. The latter relates to a comparison of Cash, Short Term Government Securities, and Receivables with current liabilities.

Another affirmative covenant is concerned with the frequency with which balance sheets, profit and loss statements, and other essential financial data are presented. Frequently, this is as often as quarterly, seldom is it less than semi-annually. More will be said about this when we discuss the procedure of following the loan after it is made.

Other affirmative covenants are more or less routine in character. They have to do with maintenance of property in good condition, proper insurance of assets, and right of access to the books of account.

One of the most important negative covenants in an unsecured loan is an agreement not to pledge any property not already hypothecated at the time the loan agreement is entered into. This is commonly called a negative pledge clause. This is usually accompanied by an agreement not to dispose of all or substantially all of the assets.

In the case of moderate sized and/or closely owned companies, it is usually agreed to that no material change in the management or in the basic character of the business which does not meet with the lender's approval will be permitted during the life of the loan. While it can be contended logically that the setting of an adequate working capital obviates the necessity for the following conditions, they nevertheless are quite generally included:

A ceiling on expenditures for fixed assets;

A limitation on the payment of dividends;

In the case of moderate sized and/or closely owned companies, on the aggregate of executive compensation;

A prohibition on the retirement or reclassification of capital stock.

A restriction on advances and guarantees or other financial commitments.

Two other negative covenants are usually found. One limits the amount of money debt which can be incurred outside of the agreement. The other has to do with commissions of acts of bankruptcy or the filing of any liens against the borrower's assets which liens are not bonded or contested in good faith within a specified period of time.

This leads to the question of the rights of the lender in the event of the default of the borrower, i.e., the breach of any warranty or the violation, without prior written consent of the lender, of any affirmative or negative covenant. The customary privilege which the lender has is to pre-mature the unpaid balance of the loan – that is, to declare the portion of the loan outstanding at the time of the default due payable immediately. Even though this right of pre-maturity, in the event of a default, is a powerful weapon in the hands of the lender it must not be confused with the ability to actually *collect* the loan at the time when it is called.

Indeed if the violation of the loan agreement is a serious one, that is probably the most persuasive argument against the ability of the borrower to repay the balance of the debt at the time that the then deferred payments are declared due and payable. What, then, is the real value of the prematurity clause? It is to give the lender the right to review his position with four possible courses of action in mind. The first is to reset the loan which, in essence, means that future payments are reduced in amount and extended in time so that schedule reimbursements correspond more nearly with the borrower's ability to meet the new level of reductions out of a lower level of income. A second resort might be to convert a previously unsecured loan to a secured basis having in mind, of course, the provisions of the bankruptcy act relating to obtaining a preferred position within four months of the institution of legal proceedings. The third alternative would be to pressure the company into some form of legal reorganization which might result in a reclassification of and legal ranking of all the company's debts. If none of these alternatives seems proper, then as a last resort, the banker may be forced to think, albeit reluctantly, in terms of a forced liquidation or sale of the business. These four means of redress emphasize the importance of setting the financial bench marks in the term loan agreement at a sufficiently high level so as to give the banker a chance to review the credit in an orderly fashion in the event of a default.

With respect to prepayment provisions, there are normally three requirements. Payments prior to schedule maturities are usually broken down into two categories – required and voluntary. Required prepayments are apt to result from a percentage of profits over and above the level necessary to meet stated maturities. The second source of required prepayments may result from the sale of fixed assets above a given amount. Prepayments from these two required soures are generally applied to maturities in inverse order of maturities and are permitted without any penalty for the anticipation. Voluntary prepayments generally are generated from borrowing obtained through sources other than the originating bank, whether publicly or privately placed.[1] On such anticipations, it is customary to provide for a premium on either a constant or a scale-down basis. The latter arrangement means that the earlier in the life of the loan, the higher is the voluntary prepayment penalty; the later in the term of the loan, the smaller is the prepayment penalty.

It cannot be emphasized too strongly that important as a properly negotiated and well drawn loan agreement is, this instrument of itself does not assure the goodness of the credit. In the final analysis it is the integrity, capability and ingenuity of the management which determines this vital matter. Having appraised the risk and having negotiated an acceptable term loan agreement, the next and final step is following the loan after it is made.

It is generally the duty of the credit department to see that financial data are received as specified in the loan agreement. It is their further obligation to see that the fiscal landmarks stipulated in the loan agreement are being followed. It is the responsibility of the loan officer to discuss with management when stipulations have not been adhered to, to determine how serious these differences may be; to agree or to disagree with proposed or actual

[1] Pre-payments out of funds generated by straight equity, as distinct from debt, financing are generally permitted without penalty.

deviations from the original terms; to see to it that corrective steps are taken if variances have been substantial, and to determine what course of action should be taken if, in his opinion, the credit demands re-appraisal. This, as a matter of fact, is his obligation even if there has been no breach in the agreement in the event that he senses the borrower's affairs are heading in the wrong direction in a significant manner.

These then are the three phases in arranging an intermediate credit. The first is the appraisal of the credit risk per se in the light of its own history and prospects, as against the backdrop of its industry and taking into account the position of the industry vis-a-vis actual or potential competitive industries. Secondly comes the negotiation and preparation of a term loan agreement which does not unduly hamper management in its daily decisions but which affords the lender reasonable protection. The third essential step is following the loan after it is made, in order to see that agreed conditions are being lived up to and to endeavor to detect significantly adverse trends soon enough so that they may be corrected before serious danger develops.

Competitive sources of intermediate credit

By now terms have been defined, the historical development of intermediate credits in American commercial banks has been put in perspective, and there has been a brief discussion of the techniques involved in making and following term loans. At this point it would be satisfying (or would it?) if the American banks could sit back and believe they had this field all to themselves. Such is not the case. Whether this be fortunate or not is a matter of opinion.

In any event, the commercial banks do have competition, some serious when measured by comparative volume and some which, up to now at least, has not been too important.

Quantitatively, the more important competitive sources are:

American industry itself;

Life insurance companies;

Profit-sharing, Pension and other Private Funds;

Factors and Finance companies.

The less important sources in volume are:

Government Business Lending Agencies;

Various Local, Regional or State Development corporations.

The least important competitors will be disposed of first.

With respect to Government Lending Agencies, let it be said here that business loans are defined in this paper as loans whose proceeds are paid directly to business. This would rule out of consideration the relatively huge volume of Government-guaranteed loans to individuals under the F.H.A. and V.A. programs. Such loans do indirectly benefit business, as do all loans, whatever the source. The funds borrowed under all loans, no matter that instrumentality makes them, ultimately go into the payment for goods or services currently being purchased or which have been acquired previously. However, a more commonly accepted definition of business loans would describe them as loans made directly to a business enterprise which receives and spends the money involved.

If this definition be accepted, then loans by Federal Agencies to business as of June 30, 1959 amouted to $5.8 billion, by the most liberal interpretation, broken down as follows:[1]

Loans to Industry	717	million
Loans to Financing Institutions	1,539	"
Loans by Export-Import Bank	3,504	"

When this total is compared with the total commercial loans of all insured banks as of June 10, 1959 of some 34 billion dollars[2] it can be realized that the inroads of Federal Lending agencies into the direct business lending field have not been significant.

As for the activities of the various development corporations which have sprung up over the past several years, despite the good work which they have done for their various communities, it is not believed that their contribution to long term capital, be it through loans or equity, has been important as yet in the aggregate.[3]

[1] *Federal Reserve Bulletin*, April 1960. p.408.

[2] *Federal Reserve Bulletin*, April 1960, p. 390.

[3] Development Corporations, as the phase is used in this context, had their inception in the United States several years ago. They are organized by groups of civic

When it comes to the major competitive sources of intermediate credit, the story is different. One of the largest of these is American industry itself. For the eight years ending 1959 (1958 figures were estimated and 1959 were projected), American nonfinancial corporations (excludes banks, insurance companies and investment companies but includes finance companies) had retained some $66 billions in earnings and had accrued $133 billions in depreciation. This makes a total of $199 billions accumulated from internal sources. To this should be added the sum of $69 raised for long term capital divided as follows: $52 billion in debt issues of one sort or another, and $17 billion as equity. These aggregate funds of $268 billion were used either to acquire or expand fixed assets in the amount of $210 billion. The remainder of $58 billion, subject to minor discrepancies, went to build net working capital.[1] In other words, of this vast expansion of assets, about 75% was financed through internal sources. Some 25% of the increased asset ownership was acquired through external means, debt and equity issues combined. This, of course, is a healthy situation and is characteristic of the method by which American business has financed its asset growth.

A second major source of long term funds for business is the life insurance companies of the United States. For the last several years their net investable funds have been running between $5 and $6 billion per annum. At the end of 1959 their holdings of business securities totaled close to $49 billion. Forty-five billion of this total was represented by debt securities and 4 billion by equities. Their interest in the business sector has developed much more rapidly than has their holding of most other types of assets. This is evidenced by the following table:

minded people, business men, bankers and others active in the affairs of the com munity to be served. Typically such companies are not interested in profits primarily. Their main objectives are twofold:

1. To induce industries to locate in the area covered by the development
2. To persuade businesses which are considering moving elsewhere to remain in the community.

As a part of these activities many of the development corporations may offer to assist (directly or indirectly) a given industry to augment its own financial resources, usually by way of long term loans, occasionally by raising equity funds.

[1] Roy S. Reierson, *The Investment Outlook for 1959* (New York: Bankers Trust Co., 1959), tables 5 and 7.

TABLE 5

	Total Assets	Gov't Securities	Business[1] Securities	Mortgages	Real Estate	Policy Loans	Other Assets
	(Figures in Millions)						
Dec. 31, '52	73,375	12,905	31,515	21,251	1,903	2,713	3,088
Dec. 31, '59	113,626	11,536	48,908	39,299	3,670	4,605	5,608
Increase or Decrease	+40,251	−1,369	+17,393	+18,048	+1,767	+1,892	+2,520

Thus, of the increase in life insurance company holdings over the past seven years, not far from 45% has taken place in business securities.[2]

Another increasing source of both medium and long term money for business (debt and/or equities) is comprised of pension profit sharing and philanthropic funds. Organizations in these categories are estimated to have added to their holdings of corporate securities some $23 billion between 1952 and 1959 inclusive. Once again the total includes securities bought in the open market.[3] [4] It should be pointed out that because of the longer term nature of the liabilities of both life insurance companies and pension funds, and the comparative accuracy with which the incidence of these debts can be forecast, these investors tend to be more interested in longer term investments than in either short or intermediate maturities. Hence, in many instances, joint arrangements have been entered into between banks and either insurance companies or pension funds. For instance, if a bank were approached for a 15 year loan and if it were satisfied with the credit, it might well decide that it would prefer to confine its participation to notes with maturities of no longer duration than five years. The bank, then, would take the initiative in obtaining a commitment with an institutional investor to take up the maturities beyond the first five years.

[1] This includes securities purchased in the open market as well as those loans which are negotiated directly with the insurance companies.

[2] *Federal Reserve Bulletin*, April 1960, p.399.

[3] *The Investment Outlook for 1959*, Table 8.

[4] A study has recently been completed of pension and profit-sharing funds under the auspices of the National Bureau of Economic Research. This survey has been conducted under the direction of Professor Roger Murray, of the Graduate School of Business at Columbia University. The results have not at the time of this writing been published.

Individual buyers are another important source of capital funds for business. These investors added some $13 billions of corporate securities to their portfolios in the eight years ending 1959.[1]

Commercial Finance companies and Factors ordinarily are thought of as suppliers of short term funds to business enterprises. Yet, because of the revolving nature of their arrangements with their clients, they may be regarded as an added source of long term funds (in fact if not in form). While it is true that if their advances against or purchases of accounts receivable are terminated, their funds are normally recoverable in a relatively short period of time, so long as their relationships with their clients continue uninterrupted, the latter have a continuous source of funds available to them. Incidental to these operations in receivables, the finance companies and factors will occasionally make direct long term loans to their clients, usually on a mortgage or chattel loan basis. The extent of the funds made available through these two media is difficult to determine and is not believed to be significant in amount.

Before leaving the discussion of competitive sources, at least passing mention should be made of two relatively new devices for either providing business with capital funds or minimizing their need for direct borrowings. The first of these plans is known as a "sale and lease-back." Under such an arrangement an industrial or mercantile company would arrange to sell its real estate and buildings to an investor, say, a life insurance company, and simultaneously lease it back from the purchaser. One important effect of this transaction is to turn these fixed assets into cash, thus adding to the lessee's liquid funds.

The second mechanism relates to the user leasing, rather than buying, income-producing equipment. When this route is chosen, the lessee is obligated to make little or no capital outlay. He pays for the use of the equipment through the periodic rental charge, usually on a monthly basis.

From the user's point of view, whether or not it is more economic to own or to lease depends on a variety of factors. Among the more important of these are the incidence of taxation, the cost of the capital involved, and the effects on the balance sheet. As far as the banks are concerned, generally speaking, they can not legaly own

[1] *The Investment Outlook for 1959*, Table 8.

capital assets except for their own use. Hence, they can not act as lessors. They can, however, finance the lessors by lending against the security of the lease. The aggregate of loans of this type up to the present time is not believed to be large.

While the growth of term loans in the commercial banking field has been substantial, there are important other sources of business funds in the intermediate and long term field. The more important of these are the internal resources generated by American industry, life insurance and pension funds, private investors and factors and finance companies. In latter years two new devices have come on the scene. These are the sale and lease back of real estate and plant and the lease of equipment. Banks can participate in these lease arrangements only in an indirect way. In other words, because of banking statutes, they may lend against the assignment of the leases as security. They can not, however in the main, be owners of real estate, buildings or machinery which is to be used by third parties.

Questions of policy

A review of the ground covered thus far substantiates the opinion that the appetite of American business for medium term loans has been growing and that the commercial banks have played their part in satisfying this demand. The acquisition of obligations of a tenor which does not conform to the traditional concept of commercial banking and in an ever increasing volume has raised certain questions with respect to lending policies. These issues have been brought up by day by day management of commercial banks as well as by serious and respected students of the American banking scene.

One basic practical consideration to be resolved by a bank not already engaged in this field is the competence of its staff to appraise intermediate credits. The judgments involved tend to lean more in the direction of investment banking than they do towards the short term "movement of goods" concept.

A second decision to be reached organization-wise involves the advisability of setting up specialized divisions to consider applications from certain designated industries which habitually have need for medium term and/or capital funds. Thus some of the larger banks have one or more of the following segregations:

Petroleum;

Transportation – including air lines and air plane or parts manufacturers;

Utilities;

Finance companies.

Also, conditions in the money market of necessity must influence bank lending policies in this, as well as in other areas concerned with the management of banking assets. Depending on how plentiful free reserves may be, the attitude of commercial banks will generally lie somewhere between being receptive to applicants for term loans to aggressively seeking such borrowers. As it was previously pointed out, the substantial excess reserve position existed in 1933 and for a number of years thereafter was one of the important influences which led to the inception and growth of intermediate credits in American commercial banks.

In addition to determining attitudes in general, easy money conditions affect banking judgment in several specific directions. Rates to be quoted is one obvious sector. Final maturities is another. When loanable funds are in good supply, schedule payments may well stretch out over a fairly long period of time, with the final maturity being as much as even ten years away. There is also a device by which the time of ultimate payment may be extended in fact, though not perhaps in form. This is accomplished by providing in the loan agreement that the last payment due will be what, in the vernacular, has come to be known as a "balloon note." When this technique is employed, spaced payments over the ostensible life of the loan are not sufficient to extinguish the entire amount originally advanced by the terminal due date. Somewhere, say, between 25% to as much as 50% of the funds provided in the first instance might be included in the last note specified in the loan agreement. This procedure applies generally to loans with an original final maturity of not over, say, five to six years.

When excess reserves are either close hauled or negative, the other side of the coin appears. Banks shun requests for term loans unless, in a given case, there are strong and compelling reasons why such an application must be considered. Among such motives might be an old and substantial relationship with the would-be borrower or even the opportunity to acquire an unusually attractive new client. Rates, of course, will be firm, maturities shortened, "balloon" payments frowned upon, and credit standards raised.

While the reasons for these shifts in policy are completely logical to the banker, unless the matter is clearly and patiently explained to the business man, understandably enough, he might easily become confused.

Before leaving the discussion of the effect which money market conditions may exert on lending policies, two other points should be touched upon. The first has to do with the basis on which rates of interest on term loans are fixed. The second concerns the analysis of an individual bank's position as distinct from the condition of the banking system as a whole.

With respect to the interest charge, when demand is strong and rates are firm, it is natural that banks should seek to fix the return to be realized over the life of the transaction, on the intermediate loans which they are making rather than to arrange the rate on a fluctuating basis. After all, if the borrower were to raise the funds by going into the public market, the cost to him to maturity would be set at the time of the underwriting, regardless of subsequent changes in the price of money. On the other hand, when the level of rates is believed to be on the low side, lenders endeavor to set the interest charge at some agreed differential above the so-called "prime" bank rate, say, $\frac{1}{4}$ to $\frac{1}{2}$ % or even more above the so-called "prime" rate. This phrase, as it is used in this context, refers to the interest which a bank would charge its very best clients on their short term – three to six months – notes. When this method is incorporated in a loan agreement, it is at times necessary to also include an agreed "floor" (a point below which the rate can not fall) and "ceiling" (a level above which the rate can not rise) as a protection for both borrower and lender. Whether the return on a particular loan is fixed or moving is determined by negotiation and in the light of competitive conditions as they exist at the time.

All that has been said thus far in this consideration of policy matters applies to banks in general. What of the position to be adopted by one individual bank? This is a question, and a serious one it is, too, to be answered by senior management acting in concert with the board of directors. Among the factors which they must take into account are the following:

The seasonal and cyclical fluctuations which are likely to occur in their deposit liabilities.

The proportion which exists between their demand and their time deposits.

The percentage of their deposits represented by outstanding loans as broken down my maturities.

The relationship between their free capital funds and their so-called "risk assets," i.e., Capital, Surplus and Undivided Profits less Banking Premises, as compared with the total of Loans, Discounts, Mortgages, and Securities other than U.S. Government Bills, Notes and Bonds.

The amount of their present outstanding term loans, revolving credits, and firm unfilled commitments under such agreements.

The quality and the scheduled maturities of their bond account.

It should also be pointed out that their decisions can not be reached in a vacuum. Competitive conditions must also be weighed in the balance even though such considerations can not be of overriding importance.

As important as specific policy decisions are, of even greater interest, perhaps, to serious observers of the American commercial banking scene, be they practitioners or academicians, are the two following broad questions:

(1) Has the increase which has already taken place in longer term loans (commercial, consumer and real estate) tended to impair the liquidity of the privately owned and privately operated commercial banking system?

(2) Has the growth in intermediate and long term credit substantially interfered with the willingness and the ability of the commercial banks to perform their classical function, which is to meet the short term seasonal needs of business, be the borrower large or be he small?

Perhaps as good a point of departure as any for this phase of our discourse is to look at a series of balance sheets and operating data for the commercial banking system as a whole. The three dates selected are December 31, 1933, 1939 and 1959. The first is picked not only because it marks the approximate date of the turn from the ravages of the Great Depression but because it also portrays the commercial banking situation at about the time of the introduction of formalized intermediate credits to American banks; 1939 is selected in order to project the banking data before the financial impact of World War II. To bring the story closely down to date, it is of course essential and interesting to include the showing for 1959. The figures are presented first in dollar amounts to indicate absolute growth. Secondly, they are presented in terms of percentages (Balance sheets, Total Assets = 100%; Earnings statements, Gross Earnings = 100%) to show the vital changes that have occurred relatively in the composition of earning assets, of liabilities, as well as in income, expenses and earnings.

A review of tables 6, 7, 8, and 9, which follow, permits some specific conclusions and lays a basis for the answers to our two main policy questions. Between 1933 and 1939 there was an expansion in member bank assets of over $21 billion, or of close to 65%. Of this increase almost 62% went into cash assets and another 33% into Government securities. Only some 5% was represented by loans.

On the liability side of the balance sheet, 87% of the increased assets, comparing 1939 with 1933, were reflected in demand deposits and 16% in time deposits. This figure of 103% is brought down to 100% by minor adjustments in other liabilities combined with a 2.6% increase in capital. At this stage of the game – i.e., on December 31, 1939 – loans amounted to less than 30% of deposits and just about 2½ times capital.

About two-thirds of deposit liabilities were offset by cash and U.S. Government securities. By any reasonable standards the banking system was too liquid. A further reflection of this condition will be found when operating figures are explored.

In the last 20 years substantial changes have, of couse, occurred. Since 1939 member banks' total assets have grown from $55 billion to over $205 billion, or about 270%. This time some 55% of this expansion has gone into the loan portfolio, 16% in cash assets, and a little better than 20% in Government's. Demand deposits account for 62% of the increase and time for 28%. Loans amount to 50% of deposits, as contrasted with 30% in '39. In the '59 figures loans are better than 5½ times capital as against 2½ times 20 years earlier.

When it comes to the breakdown of the loan figures, before application of reserves, all three classes of intermediate and long term credit (consumer loans, medium term commercial loans and real estate loans) had grown from a total of $7 billion to close to $59 billion. By 1959 these three groups absorbed about 63% of total loans. This contrasts with the estimated 50% figure which held true in 1939. Commercial term loans per se had jumped from an estimated $1½ billion to approximately $14 billion.[1]

The results of these shifts in earning assets are clearly observable from an examination of Tables 8 and 9. In 1929 interest accounted for 65% of total income. By 1939 it had dropped to 43%. In 1959 it had recovered to 62%. Income from securities which in both 1933 and 1939 stood at 34%, had dropped to 23% in 1959.

Reference was made earlier in this paper to three theories of bank liquidity – the classical – the shiftability – and the anticipated income. As far as shiftability is concerned, it is clear that the final resource in this respect is the central bank. Our study has demonstrated that the American banks have been moving substantially away from adherence to the classical approach in the direction of the concept of anticipated income. In Mr. Hayes' address to the New Jersey Bankers Association on May 19, 1960, previously referred to in the footnote, he comments as follows: "In itself, this (i.e., the steady growth in term loans) is not necessarily questionable and, in fact, the development of the term loan in the past quarter century has undoubtedly filled a very real need in the field of corporate finance; but I do believe we should avoid a situation in which banks become so heavily committed in the form of long term advances that they can not adequately meet the legitimate short term needs for which commercial banking characteristically provides rather unique facilities.

[1] It is believed that this estimate is low. Since the Federal Reserve made their most recent survey in 1957, the percentage of business loans represented by term loans has probably increased from the 38% then prevailing. In a recent address before the New Jersey Bankers Association, Alfred Hayes, President of the Federal Reserve Bank of New York, expressed the opinion that term loans of the New York City banks might represent as much as 50% of their commercial loans.

"... When the banks take on large amounts of such longer term loans they may find that they have less opportunity to meet the short term needs of smaller borrowers who have fewer open alternatives for raising funds."

In commenting on Mr. Hayes' address, B. Haggott Beckhart, Professor of Banking at the Graduate School of Business at Columbia University, in a letter to The New York Times under date of May 26, 1960 says that "an effort should be made to match the maturity of assets with that of liabilities." It is his contention that either the longer term assets should be reduced or the longer term liabilities be increased. Moreover, he commends for the consideration of the American banks a technique long used by the Swiss banks and employed recently in both Belgium and Holland. This practice consists of the banks issuing debentures with maturities running from three to eight years and at appropriate rates of interest.

The drastic shift in the nature of the earning assets of banks which has occurred over the past 20 years or so has raised important questions for senior bank management as well as for competent students of our banking system. The major broad issue concerns the influence which the growth of intermediate credit has had on bank liquidity. As a corollary what effect, if any, has this development had on the willingness and ability of the commercial banks to meet short term credit needs of worthy borrowers? It is felt here that up to this time liquidity has not been impaired and that banks generally have been satisfying short term requirements as well. However, it is also believed that both questions demand careful and continuing scrutiny.[1]

Possible future developments

Our journey together is nearing its end. We have defined terms, traced historical developments, talked about techniques, discussed competitive sources for intermediate and long term funds, and raised some questions of policy. As interesting as looking backward might be, looking forward is even more exciting albeit more hazardous. It is taken for granted that intermediate credits with commercial banks have become an accepted and acceptable

[1] For those interested in a more detailed discussion of policy, Chapters 15 and 16 of *Business Loans of American Commercial Banks* are recommended.

Table 6

Assets and Liabilities of All Member Banks
(Amounts in Millions of Dollars) (a)

	12/30/33	12/30/39	Increase or Decrease	Percentage changes from '33	Percentage Distribution of changes	12/31/59	Inc. or Decrease from 1939	Percentage change from '39	Percentage Distribution of Changes
Cash and Cash Items	6,471	19,782	+13,311	+205.7%	+61.7%	43,509	+23,727	+119.9%	+15.9%
U.S. Gov't. Obligations	7,254	14,328	+ 7,074	+ 97.5	+32.9	46,813	+32,485	+226.7	+21.6
Other Securities	5,132	5,651	+ 519	+ 10.1	+ 2.4	16,287	+10,636	+188.2	+ 7.1
Total Securities	12,386	19,979	+ 7,593	+ 61.3	+35.3	63,100	+43,121	+215.8	+28.7
Loans on Securities	4,898	1,546	− 3,352	− 68.4	−15.6	12,084(e)	+10,538	+681.6	+ 7.0
Commercial & Agricultural Loans Regular (c)	5,576	5,072	− 504	− 9.1	− 2.3	25,948	+20,876	+411.6	+13.9
Consumer Loans	N/A	2,888	+ 2,888	–	+13.4	22,480	+19,592	+678.4	+13.0
Commercial Loans– Intermediate (est.)	N/A	1,499(b)	+ 1,499	–	+ 7.0	13,994(d)	+12,495	+766.8	+ 8.3
Real Estate Loans	2,359	2,957	+ 598	+ 25.4	+ 2.8	22,185	+19,228	+616.4	+12.8
	12,833	13,962	+ 1,129			96,691	+82,729	+594.8	+55.0
Less Reserves	N/A	N/A	N/A			1,912	− 1,912	–	− 1.5
Total Loans	12,833	13,962	+ 1,129	+ 8.8	+ 5.3	94,779	+80,817	+578.9	+53.5

Customers' Liability on Acceptances	459	108	− 351	− 76.5	− 1.6	4,339	+ 2,701	+164.9	+ 1.9
Bank Premises	981	924	− 57	− 5.9	− .3				
Other Assets	699	606	− 93	− 13.3	− .4				
Total Assets	33,829	55,361	+21,532	+ 63.6	100.0	205,727	+150,366	+271.6	100.0
U.S. Gov't.Deposits	967	761	− 206	− 21.3	− 1.0	4,504	+ 3,743	+490.5	+ 2.5
Inter-bank Deposits	3,357	9,410	+ 6,053	+180.3	+ 28.1	15,048	+ 5,638	+ 53.5	+ 3.6
Other Demand Deposits	14,585	27,522	+12,937	+ 88.6	+ 60.2	110,989	+ 83,467	+303.3	+ 55.5
Demand Deposits	18,909	37,693	+18,784	+ 99.4	+ 87.3	130,541	+ 92,848	+246.3	+ 61.6
Time Deposits	8,258	11,647	+ 3,389	+ 41.0	+ 15.7	54,165	+ 42,518	+365.1	+ 28.3
Total Deposits	27,167	49,340	+22,173	+ 81.2	+103.0	184,706	+135,366	+274.3	+ 89.9
Borrowings	155	3	− 152	−	− .7	4,757	+ 4,258	+853.3	+ 2.8
Acceptances	492	124	− 368	− 74.8	− 1.7				
Other Liabilities	1,053	372	− 681	− 64.7	− 3.2				
Total Liabilities	28,867	49,839	+20,972	+ 72.6	+ 97.4	189,463	+139,624	+280.1	+ 92.7
Capital Accounts	4,962	5,522	+ 560	+ 11.3	+ 2.6	16,264	+ 10,742	+194.5	+ 7.3
Liabilities & Capital	33,829	55,361	+21,532	+ 63.6	+100.0	205,727	+150,366	+271.6	100.0

N/A Not available

(a) *Banking & Monetary Statistics* pp. 72-75; also *Federal Reserve Bulletin*, May 1960, pp. 520-521.
(b) Estimated at 26% of Commercial Loans. See page 105 of this paper.
(c) Commercial Loans less estimated Intermediate Loans.
(d) Estimated 38% of Commercial Loans. See p. 106 of this paper.
(e) Includes Loans to Financial Institutions.

TABLE 7

Assets and Liabilities of All Member Banks
Total Assets = 100% (a)
(Totals will not necessarily prove because of rounding)

	12/30/33	12/30/39	12/31/59
Cash and Cash Items	19.1	35.7	21.2
U.S. Government Obligations	21.4	25.9	22.8
Other Securities	15.2	10.2	7.9
Total Securities	36.6	36.1	30.7
(d)			
Loans on Securities	14.5	2.8	5.9
Commercial and Agricultural Loans (Regular) (est.) (c)	16.5	9.2	12.6
Consumer Loans	N/A	5.2	10.9
Commercial Loans – Intermediate (est.)	N/A	2.7(b)	6.7(e)
Real Estate Loans	7.0	5.3	10.8
			46.9
Less Reserves	N/A	N/A	1.0
Total Loans	38.0	25.2	45.9
Customer's Liability on Acceptances	1.4	.2	
Bank Premises	2.9	1.7	2.2
Other Assets	2.0	1.1	
Total Assets	100.0	100.0	100.0
U.S. Government Deposits	2.9	1.4	2.3
Inter-bank Deposits	9.9	17.0	7.3
Other Demand Deposits	43.1	49.8	54.0
Demand Deposits	55.9	68.2	63.6
Time Deposits	24.4	21.0	26.2
Total Deposits	80.3	89.2	89.8
Borrowings	.5	–	
Acceptances	1.5	.2	2.3
Other Liabilities	3.1	.7	
Total Liabilities	85.2	90.1	92.1
Capital Accounts	14.8	9.9	7.9
Liabilities & Capital	100.0	100.0	100.0

(a) *Banking & Monetary Statistics* pp. 72–75; also *Federal Reserve Bulletin* May 1960, pp. 520–521.
(b) Estimated at 26% of total commercial loans. See p. 105 of this paper.
(c) Total commercial loans – less amounts estimated as intermediate loans.
(d) Figures on loan breakdown not strictly comparable because of changes in loan classifications which have occurred from time to time.
(e) Estimated at 38% of total commercial loans. See p. 106 of this paper.

TABLE 8

Member Bank Earnings (a)
(Amounts in Millions of Dollars)
(Totals will not necessarily prove because of rounding)

	1929	1933	1939	1959
Interest and Discount on Loans	1,563	604	560	5,021
Interest and Dividends on Securities	473	426	444	1,843
Other Earnings	362	207	291	1,210
Total Earnings	2,398	1,237	1,295	8,074
Salaries and Wages	464	306	396	2,118
Interest on Deposits	759	288	159	1,280
Interest on Borrowed Money	64	15	–	–
Taxes	112	58	85	
Other Expenses	284	192	255	1,531
Taxes – Other than Income				211
Total Expenses	1,683	859	895	5,140
Net Current Earnings	715	378	400	2,934 (b)
Net Recovery or Loss on Loans	– 115	– 397	– 53	– 216 (c)
Net Profit, Recovery or Loss on Securities	–	– 265	+ 28	– 653
Other Profits or Losses	– 44	– 72	– 28	– 32
Taxes on Net Income	N/A	N/A	N/A	– 776
Net Recovery, Profit or Loss	– 159	– 734	– 53	–1,677
Net Profit or Loss	+ 556	– 354	+ 347	+1,257

(a) *Banking & Monetary Statistics*, pp. 262–263; also *Federal Reserve Bulletin*, May 1960, p. 475.
(b) Before Income Taxes.
(c) Includes Debits and Credits to Valuation Reserves and Undivided Profits.

TABLE 9

Member Bank Earnings and Other Operating Ratios (a)
Total Earnings – 100%

(Totals do not necessarily prove because of rounding)

	1929	1933	1939	1959	
Interest and Discount on Loans	65.2%	48.8	43.3	62.2	
Interest and Dividends on Securities	19.7	34.5	34.3	22.8	
Other Current Earnings	15.1	16.7	22.4	15.0	
Total Earnings	100.0	100.0	100.0	100.0	
Salaries & Wages	19.3	24.8	29.9	26.2	
Interest on Deposits	31.7	23.3	12.3	15.9	
Other Current Expenses	19.2	21.4	26.8	19.0	
Taxes other than Income	N/A	N/A	N/A	2.6	
Total Expenses	70.2	69.5	69.0	63.7	
Net Current Earnings	29.8	30.5	31.0	36.3	(b)
Net Recovery or Loss on Loans	– 4.6	–32.1	– 4.1	– 2.7	(c)
Net Profit, Recovery or Loss on Securities	–	–21.4	+ 2.1	– 8.1	(c)
Other Profits or Losses	– 1.8	– 5.8	– 2.1	– .4	
Taxes on Net Income	N/A	N/A	N/A	– 9.6	
Net Recovery, Profit or Loss	– 6.4	–59.3	– 4.1	20.8	
Net Profit or Loss	23.4	–28.6	26.9	15.5	
Ratios to Total Capital Accounts					
Net Current Earnings	11.2	7.7	7.3	18.5	(b)
Net Charge-offs, etc.	2.4	15.0	1.0	5.4	
Net Profiits or Losses	8.8	– 7.3	6.3	7.9	
Ratios to Total Assets					
Total Earnings	5.1	3.7	2.5	4.0	
Total Expenses	3.6	2.6	1.7	2.5	
Net Current Earnings	1.5	1.1	.8	1.5	(b)
Net Charge-offs, etc.	.3	2.2	.1	.4	
Net Profits or Losses	1.2	– 1.1	.7	.6	

(a) *Banking & Monetary Statistics*, pp. 264-265; also *Federal Reserve Bulletin*, May 1960, pp. 475-477.

(b) Before Income Tax.

(c) Includes Debits and Credits to Valuation Reserves & Undivided Profit.

TABLE 9

(Continued)
Member Bank Earnings and Other Operating Ratios

	1929	1933	1939	1959
Ratios to Loans				
Interest & Discount on Loans	6.1	4.7	4.2	5.5
Recoveries on Loans	.1	.2	.4 }	.2 (Recoveries and Losses combined)
Losses on Loans	.5	3.3	.8 }	
Net Return on Loans	5.7	1.6	3.8	5.3
Ratios to Securities				
Interest & Dividends on Securities	4.7	3.5	2.3	2.8
Recoveries on Securities	.2 }	.7 (Recoveries and Profits combined)	.3 }	
Profits on Securities Sold	.7 }		1.0 }	1.0 (Recoveries, Profits and Losses combined)
Losses on Securities	.9	2.9	.9 }	
Net Return on Securities	4.7	1.3	2.7	1.8

means of business financing. The answers to two questions will be attempted. What changes, of any, in procedures appear on the horizon? What is likely to be the trend in volume? The period of time for our forward look is confined to five years. It should again be stressed that the answers are solely the author's; that at best they can only be tentative, and that future actual developments may well prove them to be wrong.

There are two trends in technique now in evidence which will bear watching. One has already been touched on in passing – namely, the leasing by business of capital assets rather than acquiring title to them. This is a subject in itself. Suffice it to say that advocates claim the following major advantages for this method:

Freeing of working capital.

The substitution from a balance sheet point of view of a contractual obligation for a direct debt.

The possibility of legitimate income tax savings if the rental payments exceed allowable depreciation.

Better servicing of the equipment.

Those who have some reservations state the following objections:

If a company's credit will support a direct term loan, this is a more economical method of financing. Rates will usually be cheaper and the lessor's legitimate profit is eliminated.

The advantage claimed for the effect on the balance sheet is more theoretical than real. If contractual obligations under leases reach a figure, which in the judgment of a qualified Certified Public Accountant is material, the latter is under obligation to disclose this fact in a comment appended to the balance sheet. Sophisticated analysts will take this into account in appraising the figures.

A similar reaction exists with respect to rental payments vs. depreciation from an income tax point of view. Both figures must bear a reasonable relationship to the useful life of the equipment. Indeed, say some, with the various accelerated methods of depreciation made available since the Internal Revenue code of 1954, in the earlier years of the transaction the lessor may be at a disadvantage.

As far as servicing goes, it is contended that a reputable manufacturer will draw no distinction, whether the machinery is leased or purchased.

In practical terms, the proper decision in a given case can only be determined after all of the factors, including, of course, the important one of relative costs, have been carefully calculated.

Because of the almost complete lack of figures, the present extent of leasing and the amount loaned by banks on assignment of such contracts is impossible to state. Since there is no base from which to start, it is equally pointless to hazard a guess as to the extent of future growth. It is the belief here that the practice will continue to expand, that loans against leases will absorb a somewhat larger portion of the bank's funds available for intermediate credits than is at present the case.[1]

The second development is even more difficult to prognosticate. Some three years ago the Congress passed legislation authorizing

[1] For those interested in pursuing this matter further, serveral excellent theses on this subject have been submitted to the Graduate School of Banking at Rutgers University.

the formation of so called Small Business Investment Corporations. These were to be privately owned but their own invested funds could be supplemented by a certain percentage of Government loans. Moreover, as an inducement to investors in such companies, certain income tax advantages were offered. The basic purpose of these Small Business Investment companies was to make available to growing companies too small to raise funds in the public markets at a reasonable cost, long term credits and/or equity capital. At first, for a variety of reasons, these companies are commonly supposed to have made but little progress. More recently, however, because of the broadening of certain procedures affecting the operations of such companies there have been several Small Business Investment corporations organized with a substantial amount of initial capital raised by public issue.

It is much too early to attempt to gauge what effect these operations may have on bank intermediate credits. It is to be hoped that these so-called capital banks will make a real contribution.

In order to have a basis for attempting to guess what the volume of term loans in the commercial banking field might be in 1965, the attached Table 10 was graciously prepared by Paul A. Volcker, Jr., Financial Economist of The Chase Manhattan Bank in New York City. The sources of the data are various issues of the Survey of Current Business published by the U.S. Department of Commerce in Washington, D.C. and the Federal Reserve Bulletin.

The more or less steady rise of business loans as a percentage of Gross National Product from 6.7% in 1949 to a percentage which hovers about 9% for '57, '58 and '59, Mr. Volcker attributes to a "catching up" after loans were unduly restricted by depression and war. "During these periods the demand for business credit was relatively low. Meanwhile the government was running large deficits. Both the liquid position of the banks after World War II and the enlarged need for commercial loans growing out of post war expansion (and inflation) were conducive to a rapid rise in business lending," says Mr. Volcker. For whatever value it may have, this paper is in agreement with this hypothesis.

Next, certain assumptions must be made with respect to possible future developments. These are the author's, not Mr. Volcker's. These hypotheses are as follows, and it should again be emphasized

TABLE 10

Business Loans of All Commercial Banks Related to Gross National Product
in Current Dollars

	1949	1950	1951	1952	1953	1954	1955	1956	1957	1958	1959
Gross National Product in Current Dollars (Billions)	258.1	248.6	329.0	347.0	365.4	363.1	397.5	419.2	442.8	444.2	482.1
Business Loans of All Insured Commercial Banks (Millions) (a)	17,333	18,529	23,714	26,279	27,444	26,683	29,622	36,004	39,429	39,976	42,700
Percentage of Business Loans to Gross National Product	6.7	6.5	7.2	7.6	7.5	7.3	7.5	8.6	8.9	9.0	8.9

(a) Average of semi-annual call dates. The definition of business loans for report purposes changed in 1959. Figures for that year are estimated on a basis consistent with old definitions.

that future events may well, if not certainly, prove them to be subject to appreciable margins of error:

(1) Gross National Product for 1960 in current dollars will be $510 billion;

(2) Gross National Product in current dollars will increase on the average at an annual rate of 5% compounded between 1961 and 1965;

(3) Business loans of all commercial banks will average 10% of Gross National Product.

(4) Term Loans (this does not include either Consumer Credit or Real Estate Mortgage loans) will average 45% of the business loans of all commercial banks.

Translating these assumptions into figures would bring us to a Gross National Product figure of the magnitude of $650 billion by the end of 1965. This would imply a business loan total of some $65 billion and a term loan total of around $30 billion. Such a figure would be about double the term loans outstanding for all member banks on October 17, 1957 the date of the latest survey conducted by the Federal Reserve Board. Let it be hoped, as it is believed, that none in this audience will remember this timidly advanced forecast five years hence. If this belief did not exist, the forward look would not have been attempted in print.

Conclusion

Of the many innovations which have come on the banking scene over the past quarter century or so, few hold greater interest for practitioners and students of both banking and finance than does the term loan. Perhaps no better note can be found to close this presentation than to quote somewhat opposing opinions by two respected authorities. Professor Beckhart on pages 420-421 Business Loans of American Commercial Banks says "Of the many varieties of business loans to be found in bank portfolios, the one which parallels growth without contributing to cyclical instability is the short term, self-liquidating loan. ...

"No distortions are introduced into the economy, no liquidity problem arises. Being short term and self-liquidating, they may be safely offset on the liability side of bank statements by swiftly moving demand deposits. It is the non-self-liquidating loan, represented by short, intermediate or long term obligations, which are apt to provoke cyclical instability. Whatever may be the nominal maturity of the underlying obligations, these loans are actually long term in nature for, in good times, they can be reduced only from the cash inflow resulting from net earnings, from depreciation or depletion allowances, or can be reduced only as they are refinanced through the flotation of securities in the open market. Under adverse circumstances, repayment may require the forced liquidation of inventories and receivables. Business activity will be adversely affected."

Among others, Professor Beckhart sent his manuscript to Roger F. Murray, S. Sloan Colt, Professor of Banking and Finance at the Graduate School of Business at Columbia University, for review and criticism. On page 421 Professor Beckhart quotes Professor Murray's reaction to the foregoing opinions. "I would argue that under most circumstances the excessive expansion of self-liquidating loans will contribute just about as much to economic instability as any other rapid expansion of bank credit. ... I am not persuaded that capital loans by commercial banks are necessarily undesirable unless, of course, the volume of them creates loan portfolio imbalances."

Which of these two highly respected opinions is more apt to be right? This question, it is hoped, will furnish a basis for lively discussion, both formal and informal during and after this session of your most interesting school.

Financing an International Concern

By P. F. S. Otten

President N. V. Philips' Gloeilampenfabrieken

Now that I may speak to you on the financing of an international concern, I must at once inform you that I shall confine myself to but a few aspects of the problem. Not only do I wish to avoid dealing with subjects which I may assume are familiar to you by virtue of your functions, but moreover the financial aspects of an international concern reveal so many variants that they cannot be summarized in a simple outline.

I shall, however, approach the subjects which arise from one central point of view, namely the continuity of the enterprise.

As I stated some years ago in my address at our general meeting of shareholders, we see as the primary objective for the enterprise the creation of useful employment that is as permanent and as extensive as possible. This implies the profit motive, for without a positive result the enterprise cannot continue to exist. The profit is no longer an end in itself, but a means of enabling the enterprise to achieve constant rationalization and expansion – in other words, a means of ensuring continuity. By this we mean the preservation and, where possible, the enlargement of the relative share of the market. All the functions in the enterprise – the technical, the commercial, the social and the financial function – must direct their policies towards this aim. With this criterion in mind I want to throw more light on a number of the financial problems occurring in an international concern. Before I proceed to do so the starting-point must be worked out somewhat more extensively.

Within the scope of its social function, the production and sale of goods and services, the creation of opportunities for employment and the earning of profit, the enterprise must continually invest capital in fixed assets such as land, buildings and machinery and in current assets such as stocks and debtors. On the other hand liquid means from the sales continuously flow into the enterprise, so that a financial circulation results. The management of the enterprise must repeatedly consider whether the money regained from the investments in capital components must, either wholly or in part, be reinvested in the same activities or whether other activities shall be started on, which in turn will give rise to a similar circulation.

In the larger enterprises, and certainly in an international concern, so many policy decisions in the technical, commercial and other spheres must continually be made that delegation of initiative and responsibility is necessary This applies particularly to our concern, in which the fundamental policy of the largest possible degree of autonomy of the national and foreign concern components has the highest priority.

However, despite this delegation of powers a single coordinated policy, outlined by the top management, must be pursued in all the components, if the concern is to be prevented from disintegrating. This means that in spite of the principle of as much autonomy as possible, all policy decisions of a structural nature must remain subject to the approval of the head office. Here I have in mind specifically such problems as management organization, investments in fixed assets, new participations, etc. Finally, delegation implies the necessity for supervision.

It is obvious that all this imposes high demands on the organization. The budgeting performs an essential function in this connection, for budgeting is the drawing-up of a plan for the enterprise for the coming period, in which for each component a task-setting assignment is fixed in mutual agreement. From the budgets of the components the "Master budget" is built up, which is submitted to the top management for approval. Having the budgets submitted for acceptance enables the top management to check and correct the proposed policy, whilst comparing the budgets with the actual results and analysing the deviations constitute the final stage.

Meanwhile we must not lose sight of the fact that budgeting is a precision instrument, which should be related only to a fairly short period. Generally a maximum of one year is taken, but such a period is too short for mapping out the fundamental policy lines. For this purpose plans covering several years are necessary. It is clear that the uncertainty as to the value of the future data determining the policy increases, the further in the future these data lie. In my opinion it is therefore advisable to estimate a maximum and a minimum value of these data for the more distant years. In this way a certain flexibility in the long-term policy results; the adaptation to the constantly changing circumstances is, as it were, prepared before the changes become current. Accordingly such plans covering several years must be reformulated at regular intervals (every year, for example), and then, every time, the expectations for the first year must be given a concrete form in the budgets, i.e. in the tasks for the components of the enterprise. When these budgets are prepared, all those details that do not fit into a long-term plan can and must be taken into account.

In this way the plans covering several years and the budgeting are complementary to each other, and together they form a unique and indispensable aid to the management in their pursuit of the objective of the enterprise.

As I have already stated, this objective includes the earning of profit, and therefore kindly allow me, also to devote some attention to the substance of this concept of profit.

The modern enterprise aims at continuity. Hence there can be no question of profit unless the production apparatus, in the sense of economic production potential, has been preserved. The profit results then as the difference between the monetary value of the sales and the replacement value of the means of production sacrificed for those sales. Accordingly these means of production must be expressed in terms of money, i.e. they must be valued. It is clear that in this valuation there can be no question of values relating to moments in the past. Only a current value concept can be used.

This valuation principle, proceeding from the objective of the enterprise, is of importance not only for determination of the profit but also for the balance sheet, since the latter has to afford an insight into the size and composition of the capital. The influence of changes in the value of the assets resulting from changes in the replacement value must not be embodied in the profit and loss account, but must be shown separately on the balance sheet.

The foregoing implies that there can also be no question of profit if the capital made available by the shareholders – the owned capital, that is – has not been preserved in the true sense, i.e. as purchasing-power. This preservation can be judged through comparison of the owned capital in the enterprise at the time when the balance sheet is prepared with the owned capital on the previous balance sheet, corrected for changes in the general purchasing-power (In this respect I am thinking of changes in the cost of living).

Recapitulating, I should like to state that there can be no question of profit until the owned capital of the enterprise has been preserved, both on the basis of the general purchasing-power and on the basis of the specific price movement of the individual means of production. This follows automatically from the objective of the enterprise.

Now that in the foregoing part of my address I have set forth the general fundamentals of administration in a more or less rough form, I should like – although strongly tempted to dwell on these points at somewhat greater length – to devote some attention to their application to the financial policy, in accordance with the subject of my introduction.

The activities expected in and desired for the coming period must be precalculated and incorporated in budgets, such as sales, production, stock, investment and profitability budgets of the various concern components. From these budgets the capital requirements for the period under consideration are then calculated and the financial function will have to meet them. This implies the necessity for coordination. The financial function acts as banker of the concern components. The financial policy, i.e. meeting the capital requirements as well as possible, must be fitted in with, and adapted to, the policies of the other functions. Conversely these other functions, in turn, will not be able to carry out their policies without taking into account the possibilities for financing the activities they plan to undertake. Hence the financing has an active aspect, namely the passing-on of capital, and a passive one, the acquisition of capital.

This latter point brings us to the typical responsibility of the financial function. On the financial markets capital is offered in many forms, each with its own characteristics, its own period of availability and its own price. The finance executive will have to make a choice such that he, too, complies with the general objective of the enterprise in the best possible way.

On account of the attention to continuity the finance executive will have to acquire the capital for a period that is grafted upon the time in which the money is tied up in the enterprise. Moreover a certain flexibility will have to be incorporated in the financing, so that the expansions and contractions of the financial circulation occurring in the course of time can be followed smoothly. The financial function will also have to promote continuity by constantly keeping access to the financial markets open, in order to ensure the possibility of acquiring new resources in the best possible way. Finally, subject to the foregoing conditions, the financing will have to be carried out as economically as possible.

The necessity to acquire the financial means for a sufficiently long period has various aspects. In the first place this implies that the different activities to be financed must not be considered separately, for it is conceivable – and in a large and expanding concern it will most certainly happen frequently – that the funds becoming available from one activity are required for another. Only when the over-all capital requirements are borne in mind can the liquidity of the enterprise be prevented from becoming jeopardized because part of the acquired capital has to be repaid before it has been released from the enterprise. Here, then, lies an important criterion for the financial policy. In the second place I want to point out that although certain amounts will be required only for a limited time, there are minimum capital requirements which will have to be met preferably by means of resources that are available permanently, but at all events for a long period. In order that this minimum can be determined, long-term plans must be made.

As regards the necessary flexibility in the financing, I can be brief. At times the flow of money through the enterprise will assume a larger volume, at other times a smaller volume, and the finance executive will have to ensure that he can follow these fluctuations. This means that he must always have reserve sources upon which to draw and, on the other hand, it implies that he will have to be able to invest or dispose of surplus means. If the enterprise continues to grow, however, this latter aspect will recede more into the background. The accent will then come to lie especially on the necessity for being able to acquire the resources necessary in the future.

In this connection I cannot too strongly emphasize the importance of good public reporting. By this I do not mean merely a reporting of what has happened in the period concluded, but also a justification of the policy pursued. Through the inclusion of surveys relating to several years – a decade, for example – the continuity in the course of affairs in the enterprise can be shown more clearly, which, coupled with an exposition as to the expected future developments and the way in which the management propose to meet this future, will enable the financial markets to form an opinion. As well as through the condition that the financial obligations incurred in the past are always discharged promptly, it is only by means of such informing of all those who are in any way interested in the enterprise that access to the financial markets can be kept open.

Finally, in connection with the future provision of capital, I wish to refer to the fact that generally it is not possible to make important financial arrangements at short notice. These require a long period of preparation, and accordingly this again entails the necessity for long-term plans, which I have already mentioned; a minimum period of several years – say, four or five – seems necessary.

As regards the last aspect of the financial policy that I mentioned, namely the costs, it should be pointed out that there are differences between the charges payable for the various kinds of capital. Consequently the total costs of financing are determined not only by the amount of capital to be acquired but also by the way in which the various kinds of capital are combined, i.e. the financial structure.

You will, no doubt, know that in recent decades borrowed capital has been cheaper for the enterprise than owned capital. One of the reasons for this phenomenon is that in the past the lenders have not realized sufficiently the adverse effects of inflation. As a result they have attached too much value to the risk-avoiding aspect of borrowed capital, which, on account of its nature of debt of the enterprise, is characterized by fixed obligations of the creditor in respect of repayment and remuneration. Therefore the lenders were prepared to accept a relatively low return.

For this reason the borrowed capital was already comparatively cheap for the enterprise. In addition, the costs of borrowed capital – unlike dividend distributions – are deductible from the taxable profit. Hence the total costs of financing can be reduced considerably through the acquisition of relatively more borrowed capital.

The difference in price between the kinds of capital mentioned also implies the possibility of increasing the earning-capacity of the owned capital, provided, at least, that the over-all earning-power of the enterprise is greater than the interest to be paid for borrowed capital. If the yield from the total capital employed in the enterprise, i.e. the profit before taxation plus the interest paid, is higher in relation to that total capital than the rate of interest to be paid for the borrowed capital, the return on owned capital will increase according as financing is carried out less with owned and more with borrowed resources.

All these considerations, which, as I shall show more clearly, gain force in an international concern owing to the inflationary development in various countries, must not, however, tempt the finance executive to acquire too large a part of the necessary resources in the form of borrowed capital. The fixed charges proceeding from these debts call for a continuous stability in the flow of income, with the result that the susceptibility to market conditions of the articles to be produced plays an important part. Here, too, the attention to continuity, which in this connection amounts to the attention to solvency, must be the guiding principle for management.

Before concluding this part of my address I wish to draw your attention once again, this time in relation to the costs of financing, to the importance of the reporting which I have already mentioned. Those who place money at the disposal of the enterprise do so with certain expectations in respect of principal and return. It is therefore of the greatest importance for them to be able to form an accurate picture of the enterprise. Too unfavourable a picture leads to an increase in the costs of financing, since the lenders assess the risk too high, whereas on the other hand steps must be taken to prevent the expectations from being too optimistic, which would result in disappointments and might cut off the financial lifeline of the enterprise.

If we now wish to apply these basic principles of the financial policy in an international concern, we encounter so many problems relating to organization and the technique of financing that I can touch upon only a few of them.

The starting-point for my thoughts is, then, that in spite of the necessity, in an international concern, to delegate an important part of the financial management to local managers, the unity in the policy must never be lost. The fundamental lines for the financial policy to be pursued must be laid down by the central management. For short-term borrowed capital, such as bank and acceptance credits, the delegation can – both as regards the choice of the form of capital and the actual conclusion of the contracts – go farther than for the acquisition of long-term borrowed capital, in the case of which the financial consequences are fixed for a much longer period. As regards the owned capital it is not possible, in principle, to delegate powers of decision, if for no other reason than the juridical parent company – subsidiary relationship.

Proceeding from the future capital requirements on the one hand and from the directives for the financial management on the other, the concern components must propose a choice from the available sources of financing. Following approval by the head office the total costs of financing can be precalculated, with due regard to the desired interrelationship between the kinds of capital and their costs. This precalculation can be used as a financial budget and, on the basis of analyses of the differences between the costs of financing actually paid and those budgeted, the efficiency of the financial policy in the concern component in question can be judged. Here I would point out, however, that if the actual amounts fall short of or exceed the budgeted costs of financing and this is not caused either by a capital structure deviating from the original financial planning or by prices of the kinds of capital deviating from those originally allowed for, the financial management of the concern component in question must not be held responsible. It is quite conceivable that, for example, functionaries in other sectors may have exceeded their budgets and so have given rise to unexpected additional capital requirements. Nor must the financial management of a concern component be held responsible for the effect on the costs of financing of financial measures prescribed by the head office.

Another important problem arising in the financial administration of an international concern is the structure of the owned capital of the subsidiaries. This can be obtained from two sources, namely either from the parent enterprise or from other suppliers of capital, through the issue of shares on the local financial market. Naturally it will not be possible for the whole of the owned capital to be acquired on the local market, since this is contrary to the concept of a concern. Here we touch upon a policy problem of the first order, which goes far beyond purely financial interest, namely the question as to the extent to which the parent enterprise must itself participate in the subsidiaries. I do not want to enter into this problem too deeply, but wish only to state that at all events an important part of the owned capital required by the subsidiaries will have to be provided by the head office. This can confront the head office of a large international concern with so great a need for capital that it can no longer be met by the capital market of the country of registration. I need hardly substantiate this statement. To mention one example, it will immediately be clear to you that it would be very difficult for a small country like the Netherlands to meet the joint capital requirements of concerns such as Royal Dutch Shell, Unilever, AKU and Philips. Should these concerns have to confine themselves to the Netherlands for their financing with owned capital, their expansion would be checked to a marked degree. It is partly for this reason that we are pleased with the favourable reception encountered by our shares on the international stock exchanges, and I can assure you that, within the scope of the objective of our concern, we shall do everything in our power to retain an extensive market for these shares. To me it seems obvious that in this respect, as well, the provision of information, to which I have referred several times, is of great importance. It seems to me to be equally clear that on account of these problems we are in favour of the greatest possible freedom of current payments and of movement of capital in the world. We accordingly welcome the liberalization of the movement of capital provided for in the E.E.C. Treaty. This liberalization will permit of a more efficient use of the available financial resources and will enable us to acquire the necessary capital, both owned and borrowed, on the cheapest markets and to assign it to those places where it is most needed.

At the same time we feel it is to be regretted that with regard to the liberalization of the movement of capital the E.E.C. follows a negative procedure, by starting from the assumption that in principle all capital transactions are prohibited and then – albeit, fortunately, at an accelerated rate – granting general licences for the various categories. We are more in favour of a positive method of approach, namely a fundamental liberalization of all movement of capital. For those countries which cannot as yet free certain transactions the possibility for making exceptions must then be left open for the time being, which restrictions the countries concerned would of course have to defend before an internationally constituted forum appointed for this purpose. They would have to repeat this defence periodically, in order to prevent certain restrictions from continuing to exist longer than is warranted. Thus the burden of proving the need for continuation of restrictions would rest on the countries themselves, and this appears to us to be much more effective than the current procedure, which means, in fact, that the Monetary Committee of the E.E.C. must prove that at a certain moment all six Member States are, financially and economically, in a position to liberalize certain categories of capital transactions.

Besides the liberalization of capital transactions the gradual establishment of the Common Market will also in other ways entail financial consequences for an international concern. Owing to the elimination of quantitative restrictions and import duties a larger measure of specialization in production will become possible. This will have a favourable influence on the cost prices, but in addition, it will result in a more intensive exchange of goods between the concern components.

Though it is still too early for specific statements to be made on the subject, I consider it possible that the over-all capital requirements of the concern components established in the Common Market will decrease on account of a regrouping of this kind. However, in any case the greater interchange of goods will cause a geographical shift in those requirements. The question then arises as to whether, for example, the greater export from country A to country B will have to be financed by means of suppliers' credit from A to B or whether it is more advantageous to have country B pay cash. I can also imagine that the flow of goods between A and B is financed with capital acquired in country C. Moreover, the more intensive interchange of goods may well cause the minimum point of the fluctuations in the financial requirements to become higher, which means that in the future a larger proportion of the necessary capital will have to be acquired on a long-term basis.

If the financial management wish to be able, in good time, to make an estimate as to the capital requirements resulting from the creation of the E.E.C. and as to the covering of those requirements, then again this entails the necessity for long-term planning, for a continuous analysis of the supply of capital in its various forms in the different countries and, finally, the necessity for intensive consultations between the financial managers of the concern components and the head office. Hence I expect more intensive dealings in the future between the financial managements of the concern components established in the various European Common Market countries.

Before concluding my address I should like to invite your attention to two more points.

The financial management of an international concern are continually confronted with the fact that in several countries of the world inflationary developments are taking place. This means not only that even in the case of unchanged activity the need for financial resources in such a country constantly increases, but also – and this, viewed from the aspect of the pursuit of continuity, is much more important – that special measures will have to be taken to preserve the invested capital as well as possible in the quality of actual purchasing-power. If the capital made available by the head office is invested in nominal assets, it is fully subject to the adverse influence of inflation. As a primary guide for financing it follows that, where at all possible, borrowed capital for the financing of nominal assets must be acquired locally, since this has the character of a nominal debt.

When this guide is applied the associated costs must not be lost sight of, however. In many inflation countries the level of the rates of interest is very high, since often the lenders try to calculate the inflation in the interest payable, as a result of which the acquisition of borrowed capital can become more disadvantageous than acceptance of the inflation loss.

As far as the capital is tied up in goods, whether in fixed assets or in stocks, it is comparatively immune from inflation. This does not mean to say, however, that the exchange-rate risk also is then automatically covered. If, over a certain period, the rate of exchange of the foreign currency in question falls to a greater extent than that to which the replacement value of these goods rises, the concern capital is eaten into as a result.

Here we encounter problems connected with forward transactions, swaps, etc., but since, on account of your banking-function, these will not be unfamiliar to you, I would rather not go into them further now – partly for considerations of time.

Finally I should like to call your attention to the important financial consequences of the function that an international concern can fulfil in the endeavours of the free western world to cooperate with newly developing countries in order to increase their prosperity. Who are better qualified to supply the technical equipment and the know-how required by these countries for their industrialization than the large international concerns? Naturally, many more aspects are associated with the problem of the newly developing countries than the financial one about which I am speaking to-day. For these I would refer you to my address at our last general meeting of shareholders, of which I shall have a copy placed at your disposal.

The financing of the goods and services to be supplied to these territories calls forth many problems. Generally speaking, cash payment will hardly ever be possible. On the contrary, long credit terms are demanded, and you are doubtless aware that in international competition the role of the credit period is often more important than that of the price and even that of the quality. You will also know, of course, that the so-called Berne Union was established to prevent unlimited credit competition and that recently attempts have been made to get round these agreements again by means of the so-called tied loan. It will not surprise you to hear me state that private trade and industry can and must never borrow the resources required for the financing of these credits unless proper insurance facilities are created. If these facilities remain inadequate, and should industry and commerce nevertheless have to invest in these territories via the export credits, then, owing to the nominal character of these investments, the risks involved will become greater that those resulting from the establishment of subsidiaries there.

Since the risks involved in these long-term loans or participations are, relatively, very considerable, and the return must be viewed over a long period, these risks will have to be absorbed in the financial structure of the concern through the necessary provision for them from current income.

I have now reached the end of my address. In any large enterprise, and certainly in an expanding international concern such as ours, the financial policy must be aimed primarily at the maintenance of a balanced financial structure, based on continuity, and at keeping access to the financial markets open. I hope that both your visit to-day and my introduction will contribute towards the achievement of this aim.

The Relationship Between Government Credits and Guarantees and the Credit Policy of Commercial Banks An Evaluation of a Possible Trend

By L. de Block
Managing Director K.L.M.

Since the subject I am going to discuss covers a very wide area, I plan to restrict this talk to the situation as it occurs in economically highly developed countries of the free Western world. Even in this limited area, however, there is a magnitude of forms and institutions through which the government directly or indirectly meets private credit requirements.

For simplicity's sake I will use the term government credits to include medium and long term credits and guarantees. This area of government credits is not only very extensive, but also not easy to survey. Existing credit arrangements in the various Western countries differ widely in categories of credit users, purposes of credit arrangements, and credit conditions. In this brief lecture it will be impossible for me to give a useful review of all these arrangements. I will also not indulge in the tempting challenge to compare various credit arrangements as they exist in different countries. I think that a theoretical discussion of the subject will be most useful, although I will refer from time to time to factual developments.

I would like to discuss the following three aspects:

First, why do governments interfere so frequently with the granting of credits to the private sector? I will discuss here only government credits of a *normal* and *businesslike* character granted to private enterprises which therefore have an economic objective.

Second, I would like to see how we should evaluate this form of government activity.

Third, I would like to see if the granting of government credits is indispensable in our modern society, or whether this responsibility can be taken over in full or in part by private financing companies, including commercial banks

And now the first question: why do governments participate in the granting of credits to private companies? As I have already said I will limit myself to the granting of credits of a *normal* and *businesslike* nature. I need not tell you that governments have given and still give a considerable number of credits which do not have a normal and businesslike character. Credits have been given with an outspoken political intention. For example, credits have been given against unusually favorable conditions turning these credits in fact into subsidies, to induce entrepreneurs to make certain decisions desired by the government such as the establishment of a company in a so-called depressed area. The government must sometimes act as lender of credits in times of war or other serious upheavals in cases which cannot very well be covered by private financing companies. I hope that you will allow me to exclude all such cases from my discussion as they are of minor importance from the viewpoint of the private banker. The then remaining area covers those cases where the government grants credits under normal conditions directly or indirectly (through guarantees) to enterprises to finance the normal functioning of the relevant enterprise. The financing activities of the government in such cases are generally regarded in our free Western world as unusual because as a rule capital requirements of private enterprises are covered through private financing sources. Why is it that governments make exceptions to this general rule?

I believe the answer may be summarized as follows. In the first place, there must be a demand for capital which in the government's opinion, – not necessarily that of private financing institutions, – cannot be met, at least not satisfactorily, by private financiers. Why do governments take this viewpoint? It may be because the structure of the private credit system in the relevant country shows certain *deficiencies*. It is also possible that the financing requirements are of such a nature that it is either not attractive or not easy for private credit lenders to meet these requirements. A difficulty or lack of opportunity to cover relevant financing requirements from private sources results only in government action through granting the desired credit or giving a guarantee if the government believes it is in the *public interest* to provide for these requirements.

Such an answer to the question why governments participate in financing transactions gives rise, of course, to two further questions. First, what are the *deficiencies* in the structure of the private credit system and what is the specific nature of certain financing requirements which cannot be met through private channels.

Second, what exactly is this *public interest* on which a government bases its financing intervention.

As regards the second question, it is not possible to give a clearly defined description of what is meant by public interest because opinions on whether the public interest is involved in a specific situation and if so to what extent, vary widely from country to country and within a country too. The same applies all the more to the question whether government intervention in the public interest is justified.

However, when we review practical experience we see that governments justify in general granting credits to certain private enterprises or categories of enterprises on the basis of one of the following criteria:

(1) the establishment or expansion of the relevant enterprises creates a needed increase in employment opportunities or

(2) desirably strengthens the economic potential of the country or its economic position, as when credits are granted to new basic industries or for export financing, or

(3) because the preservation and the prosperity of the relevant group of enterprises are of great importance in the interest of a healthy structure of society. Such factors play an important role in the organization and granting of financing facilities to small companies, agriculture and shipping.

After these observations about the meaning of the words "public interest," I would like to return to the other factor, deficiencies, which governments use in justifying their deviation from the principle that private financing requirements must be met by private financiers. The government's opinion is that *deficiencies* in the organization of the private credit system and special peculiarities of certain financing requirements which make it impossible for the private credit system to meet otherwise reasonable financing requirements, force the government to step in. In this regard I believe there is no question of such deficiencies in our Western countries with their highly developed private banking system, at least with respect to short term credits.

If demand for short term credits remains unsatisfied, the cause must not be sought in deficiencies of the supply mechanism but in specific aspects of relevant credit applications. However, there can be deficiencies in the way in which private financiers meet the demand for medium and long term credits needed by private industry. The circumstances differ of course from country to country. There are countries where the private banking system and affiliated institutions have been engaged for a long time in granting medium and long term credits. In other countries, including the Netherlands, there has been a tendency for many years to limit the responsibility of the private banker to the granting of specifically short term credits.

I will not deal with the granting of medium term credits because you have been informed already on the principal aspects of this subject by specialists in this field. With respect to long term credits, the business community of many countries, particularly industry, must cover its long term needs through self-financing or through a direct appeal to potential investors. As regards the latter approach, the most appropriate form is of course the issue of shares or debentures.

This possibility exists only for relatively large companies which are known to the public, or command their confidence. However, smaller companies do not have this possibility. These companies must depend on their own capital and on what can be added through plough-backs of earned profits, unless they find capital owners in their circle of relatives and friends who are capable and willing to supply sufficient amounts as private contract loans or through joining such companies as limited partners. It is not surprising that because of these deficiencies on the capital market with which small companies are confronted, many governments feel they have a duty to financial assistance.

It seems probable that the difficulties for the small entrepreneur to obtain long term capital have been considerably increased during recent decades as a result of changes in the economic and social structure. In the first place, the increase in the capital component of the production apparatus, even in small companies, has considerably enlarged their financing requirements. At the same time, changes in the social structure and the emergence of attractive alternative investment opportunities, especially through stock exchanges, have made it much more difficult for small enterpreneurs to find a "rich man" willing to supply the necessary capital. Last but not least, the tremendous increase in the tax burden further aggravates the difficulty for the small entrepreneur to reserve adequate amounts from his profits to finance consolidation and expansion of his company. This increase in the tax burden has at the same time impaired the financial status of medium size capital owners who are the traditional suppliers of capital for small entrepreneurs.

The criticism has often been heard in the Netherlands that the government's introduction of credit facilities for small enterprises no longer able to obtain the necessary funds from private sources, is an attempt to offset existing deficiencies on the capital market which the government has created itself through its fiscal policies. Although this is undoubtedly exaggerated, it cannot be denied that there is some truth in this criticism. An additional obstacle for small companies is that commercial banks and their affiliated financing companies, to the extent that they are engaged in granting medium and long term credits, frequently show little interest in granting such credits to small enterprises. This is not always without reason because a small company presents special risks since it often cannot offer adequate securities as collateral and since the chances for success depend strongly on the qualities of the owner. An extensive and relatively expensive advance investigation and continuous supervision of the company's activities are necessary to limit these risks as much as possible. This affects of course the credit yield unless a high interest rate is paid. This results in an unfavorable interaction. Because commercial banks and other financing institutions are reluctant to grant credits to small enterprises, they don't establish a special and competent apparatus to handle adequately such credit applications, this in turn aggravates their negative attitude to this type of credit granting.

Because of all these factors, the financing of small companies has become one of the areas par excellence where government credits play an important role. In addition, as I mentioned already, the preservation and prosperity of small entrepreneurs represents an important social problem which is not ignored in political circles. There is virtually no political party which does not give high priority to promoting the interests of the small businessman, the majority of small entrepreneurs.

While financing small enterprises is therefore one of the areas where government credits play a major role, governments frequently act also as financiers of very large projects. This may on the surface appear paradoxical but the explanation of government activity in these opposite sectors of credit granting is simple. Next to the small business sector stands the sector of medium-sized and normally large enterprises where possibilities for financing from private sources are much larger. These companies have access to the capital issue market, and financing institutions are also more inclined to provide funds to these companies. Their stability, their possibility to offer collateral, the knowledge of risks involved, all these factors make it much more attractive to offer credits to these categories of enterprises. Deficiencies may also occur in the credit mechanism of this sector, for example when financial institutions show little interest in the granting of medium and long term credits. However, government financing in the middle sector is not important. Government activity in this sector is also limited because the chance that governments collide with private financiers and that they will be criticized for discriminatory practices is much larger than in the above mentioned sectors. In addition, government financing in this sector is presumably less rewarding from a political viewpoint. The granting of credits to small companies concerns a group which is more influential from a social and political standpoint, while the granting of government credits to very large enterprises usually concerns very spectacular cases such as a blast furnace project or other basic industries. The establishment of such enterprises strengthens with one stroke the economic potential of the relevant country, and creates, directly and indirectly, substantial employment opportunities. Public opinion therefore tends to regard financial assistance to such spectacular projects as worthwhile, much more so than financial assistance which is given to medium-sized companies.

The financing of very large projects from private sources on the other hand, frequently causes difficulties, particularly when they are brand new and not expansions of already existing enterprises, because it is often impossible in such cases to go to the capital market as the profitability of the project has not yet been proved. About the same objection applies to banks and other financing institutions. The required capital for such projects is usually so large that even when these institutions are willing to participate in the financing, they cannot fully meet capital demand without violating their responsibility to spread their risks. So governments often act as financiers, often in cooperation with private financing institutions, in such projects.

We have seen now that government credits are especially granted to very small and very large enterprises and in particular to very large new enterprises. There is a third financing sector where governments are frequently active though government activities in this particular sector more frequently take the form of granting guarantees rather than credits. It concerns here financing requirements where unusual risks occur, in particular the financing of export transactions.

The granting of credits in this field can be handled by private banks or their affiliates, but they are only prepared to give export credits when the exporter is insured against the exchange rate risk and against the risk of non-payment by the foreign buyer either because he himself fails to pay or because the government of his country makes it impossible to transfer the purchase amount. The possibility of insuring such export credits depends in many countries on the willingness of the government to enter into guarantee for possible losses which may result from the insurance even though the insurance is sometimes formally concluded with a private or semi-private company. Although the government in these latter cases occupies from a legal viewpoint only the position of reinsurer, the granting of the export credit by the bank and of the guarantee by the government to the export credit insurer must be seen as a whole from an economic viewpoint. Although intermediaries are used, the government guarantees ultimately the repayment of the credit to the bank, and the bank is only willing to grant credit on the basis of this guarantee

Why do governments feel that the activities of private organizations in this field need supplementation? The private financer/credit insurer is in principle prepared to accept a certain risk with respect to redemptions, especially when he receives financial compensation. However, this risk must be of such a nature that the resulting losses in any given year never represent an excessive percentage of the total borrowed amount. This is because the private insurers want to reach an equilibrium or preferably a favorable balance within a reasonable time, between the losses to be paid and the premium amounts which are received for the risks involved. Governments attach very great importance to the concluding of export transactions because of the significance which governments attribute to the development of exports as the motor for economic expansion. Furthermore governments can take the risks involved even if the credit volume is very large and more so when the credit transactions are divided over a longer time period. In addition, governments only need to reach a balance between profits and losses resulting from these government guarantees; it is self-evident that this last feature is unacceptable for a private financing company.

It is possible to establish a premium on the basis of commercial standards for the normal *bad debt risk*, although in the case of export financing this risk is frequently not a normal one because the debtor is often the State or a State agency. The question is whether insurance can be contracted on this basis in view of the amount of the transaction and the level of the private premium which would have to be paid. It is not unlikely that government assistance would have to be sollicited if the transaction is to be concluded. As regards the insurance of the *political risks* involved, the governments would seem to be the appropriate insurers because of the fact that this risk is beyond computation. With respect to the *exchange risk* much depends on the currency and the period involved. Some governments assist in this field because the risk factor cannot be calculated by private persons and premiums can therefore not be established.

By and large, government activities in the field of granting guarantees and credits in competition with the banking community take place in the following three categories where as we have seen, deficiencies exist in the credit mechanism of the banking system:

(1) small credits

(2) large credits

(3) export credits.

The following question must now be answered:

Are governments the appropriate authorities to fill these deficiencies? The general objection against governments acting as credit lenders and guarantors is that governments operate in goldfish bowls. Governments carry political responsibility for their actions. The commitments which they make and their effects, must be justifiable from a budget point of view. The government's political responsibility makes them subject to Parliamentary criticism and consequently to the criticism of a not always loyal opposition and the press. Budgetary responsibility (on losses, because there will be no evidence of cash results when there are no losses) makes the results of government actions apparent in specific budget items. In addition, parliament must be consulted or at least be informed whenever governments initiate new activities or change already existing government activities. Considerable delays can be expected when changes in existing policies or the initiating of new activities require parliamentary approval of new legislation. Under such conditions it becomes very difficult to exert a a flexible policy which can quickly be adapted to changing conditions although such a flexible policy is required when governments are engaged in these activities.

Another principle of government policy is that identical cases must be treated in an identical way. However, many shades of difference are possible in the granting of credits and guarantees. For example, identical credit or guarantee applications can still represent different cases if only because of the different personalities who are involved. While the possibility of public criticism on the one hand will tend to result in great caution in order to prevent the danger of losses, the necessity of equal treatment may on the other hand result in the granting of unwarranted credits and guarantees. Governments will therefore frequently be tempted to cover up losses resulting from these transactions as long as they can and may sometimes decide to throw good money after bad money.

It will be particularly difficult for governments to realize the ideal of the granting of credits and guarantees, this ideal being to find the fine line between excess of caution and excess of zeal, and to find this line quickly and efficiently. A special point of consideration is how governments arrive at decisions concerning the granting of individual credits and guarantees.

The governments must in general consider these applications on a strictly commercial basis except in special cases, for example when the government has a different opinion than private industry on long term prospects. The competence of government officials to evaluate creditworthiness and their ability to calculate long term prospects, although probably better than is generally believed, is limited. A government official is inclined to be cautious because a correct decision raises no public attention while a wrong decision may have the most unpleasant repercussions, particularly if it becomes a political football. In addition to pursuing joint ventures with commercial institutions to guarantee a purely commercial judgment, governments can also arrive at this objective by using private advisers. The question whether and to what extent governments can delegate their authority of decision in these matters, despite the fact that they carry the responsibility for these decisions, depends on whether a government can rely on a sufficient number of objective advisers. A fortunate solution in the field of export credit insurance has for example been found in the Netherlands where government involvement has been kept to a minimum through the utilization of the services of a private company, the Netherlands Credit Insurance Company, and the assistance of the central bank. This saves the government a lot of extra work and quarantees expert treatment as well as quick action.

All this goes to show that governments are not at all the appropriate institutions to grant credits or guarantees. It seems therefore useful to explore whether government activities in the field can, entirely or in part, be shifted back to private business. There is all the more reason for this investigation because conditions under which governments operate have drastically changed, at least in Europe.

Before 1940 the granting of credits was almost entirely a matter for private business. Debtor countries covered their financing needs directly on the capital market and therefore there was only a limited need for export credits. Furthermore, there was no ideology for underdeveloped areas. In short, this was a period of individualism in government policies too. There existed in addition a certain dislike of new forms.

After 1945 we witnessed drastic government intervention in commercial relations, inevitable in the early postwar period; a frequently exaggerated interest in wiping out underdeveloped areas; an urge for cooperation in political and economic matters both in a national and an international level; and an intensive search for new forms whenever old forms were no longer satisfactory.

We must investigate whether these new tendencies have properly influenced the credit and guarantee policies of the governments or whether a reorientation of government policies in these fields is necessary. We will review from this viewpoint the three categories in which the governments primarily play a role.

Small credits (small business companies and self-employed small businessmen)

I have already indicated why governments believe that they must often play a role in granting these credits. They are motivated by the existing lack of interest in granting such credits among commercial banks where collaterals are inadequate, where too much depends on the personal qualifications of the owner of the small business company, and where excessively high costs are involved for administering and supervision. I did not mention the factor of the longer loan period since a solution can be found for this difficulty. The solving of this problem of granting term loans in the banking sector will be further facilitated as banks attract savings deposits. Dutch banks recently began to stimulate the opening of savings accounts.

The problem of high administrative costs should be surmountable now that mechanization in business administration is rapidly progressing, provided that the volume of these credits reaches a level that mechanical data processing methods can be applied. However, it will remain difficult to find a solution for the larger control expenditure items. A solution could perhaps be found through the technical cooperation with professional organizations which can prepare recommendations for the simplification and unification of accounting methods.

The experience of already granted credits must show whether alleged difficulties such as the presumed inadequacy of available collateral and the dependence on the personal qualifications of the owners of small business companies are of such dimensions that government assistance for these categories is inevitable. Exact data regarding the results of this kind of credit granting are extremely scarce. As a case in point, the results of credit granting under government guarantees in the Netherlands are most encouraging. The total loss on bad debts since 1945 on a credit volume of about $100 million amounted to only 0.6%. It is much more difficult to evaluate the results of credit operations carried out in the United States by the Small Business Administration. Bad debt losses on business loans amount to about one percent, but total results of the S.B.A. are distorted because maximum interest rates are applied to credits granted in the S.B.A. framework, and high interest rates are recently paid for funds obtained from the U.S. Treasury. The final result was a small profit margin or a small negative margin when bad debt losses are taken into account. To confuse these results still more, the fact should be mentioned that special services are supplied to debtors which increase credit costs and, consequently the end results. The bad debt losses of the National Fund for Professional Credits in Brussels, an institution which is engaged in the granting of small credits, are not published, but it appears that their losses also amount to about one percent of their total credit volume. I have no information on the bad debt losses of any other small credit institutions.

The available results indicate that the bad debt risk in small business credits granted or guaranteed by individual governments since 1945 has been low, although it must be taken into account that these results were achieved in a period of economic expansion. On the basis of these results the question should be raised whether governments still have a function to fulfill in the granting of credits in the small business sector. Alternative solutions are possible. Would it not be possible to find a solution through the establishment of cooperative credit institutions such as the Genossenschaftsbank in Germany and the cooperative agricultural credit banks in the Netherlands? This form of institution enables persons engaged in the same trade or industry to cooperate thus eliminating deficiencies in the credit mechanism. In addition, these people are better qualified to evaluate the creditworthiness of an applicant than outsiders – even those who specialize in granting small business credits.

If this type of solution seems undesirable, a form of cooperation could be created between professional organizations and the banks engaged in granting small business credits with the professional organizations granting guarantees and the banks credits. If the professional organizations found risks too high, though experience indicates that risks have so far been small, they might consider establishing a separate guarantee granting agency or utilizing the services of existing institutions in this field. There is still another reason for considering a change in the system of granting small business credits. It appears that the present centralized system for considering credit applications in the banking world is one of the reasons why the small credit borrower finds it difficult to obtain credits. At the time that the local banking system still dominated, personal factors played a more important role in decisions on credit applications, and rigid banking principles were less drastically applied. These personal factors are now the more important as one of the major obstacles which exist today is that there is more shortage of available capital rather than need for more credit applications, a factor which used to play a far less important role in the past. The introduction of personal loan facilities in recent years has again focussed attention on the importance of the applicant's personal qualifications and lowered the importance of available collateral. These new facilities would ease these difficulties and would make it easier to grant small business credits.

An earlier attempt to solve this problem was made in the United Kingdom. In this country special attention had been given on the problem, known as the Macmillan gap, since 1931 when it was found that the financing of small and middle sized business companies gave difficulties. The Charterhouse Industrial Development Company, abbreviated CID, a private institution established in 1934, and the Industrial and Commercial Finance Corporation, abbreviated ICFC, established in 1945 by the Bank of England in cooperation with several commercial banks, are both engaged in granting small business credits. However, in 1959 the Radcliffe Report showed that this problem was not solved, and suggested that banks grant term loans to small business companies.

A higher interest rate will have to be paid for small business credits in countries where government guarantee or credit granting activities in this field are abolished. On the other hand, the advantage would be that unnecessary government interference be prevented in the future.

A sounder credit system would emerge and a more realistic price for the credit facilities would be paid.

The introduction of new procedures to eliminate government interference in granting credits or guarantees in this sector will meet strong political opposition and the governments risk to be blamed for leaving the little fellow in the lurch. A try should however be made. A policy of a gradual retreat of government activity in this field may be considered if it is felt that the policy change just described would be too drastic. A transition from a government-supported to a private credit system could be facilitated if the government concerned would be prepared to grant initially a liquidity guarantee. Furthermore, if a possible shortage of risk-bearing capital available to credit applicants would occur and represent an obstacle for granting these credits, the government should be willing to assist in finding a solution.

Large credits, respectively investments

This category always consists of special cases involving large amounts, long credit periods and special risks. It is impossible in these cases to arrive at a general conclusion whether or not government assistance in the realization of these credit transactions is justified. In addition, the situation varies from country to country. For example, in countries where affiliations exist between industry and the banking system, demands for government assistance will be less readily made than in countries where such affiliations do not exist. It is in some cases certainly possible that the desired financing needs cannot be satisfied without government assistance. However, continuous efforts must be made to reduce government assistance to a minimum and to find suitable means to reach this minimum. Government assistance must be limited as much as possible to guarantee granting, and as far as possible private sources should be implemented. If the projects are too large to be financed locally, requests for financing assistance should be made to the International Bank in Washington, the European Investment Bank, or to an international syndicate of banks. This also has the advantage that a more objective judgment on the merits of the credit application can be arrived at than judgment on a national level could provide. Continuous attention must also be given to the possibility of shifting the credit portion being financed or guaranteed by the government to the private sector as soon as the risks involved and the duration of the credit period allow this.

Export credits

A system for granting and guaranteeing export credits has emerged over the years which has resulted in an extremely complicated mechanism. It would be impossible and also impractical to subject this mechanism as a whole to a critical examination. However, it is useful to study this mechanism for the purpose of separating the responsibilities which belong on the one hand to the private sector, in this case to the private banking system, and on the other hand to the government sector. Later on, it will be considered whether this separation could be realized within the framework of a revised export credit mechanism.

To the natural responsibility of the private sector/banks belong those credits whose credit period corresponds with or is shorter than that of medium term credits, and which involve sharply defined projects of a commercial nature. These credits consist of export credits in the traditional sense of the term. Further medium term financing credits of a business nature also belong in this category. The effects of certain aspects inherent in these credits such as the political risk factor will be discussed later on. The granting of credits which do not comply with the justmentioned conditions represent special difficulties, in particular when the credit period exceeds that of medium term credits or when credits belong in the category of assisting underdeveloped areas. Under such circumstances credit granting belongs within the framework of government policy. Special attention must be given in this connection to the International Bank which demonstrates a successful shift from government to private financing. Credit granting by this institution originally took place entirely with government funds. During the course of time a gradual shift to private funds financing took place although the non-fully-paid capital which the member countries contributed still serves as a guarantee.

The responsibilities of the private sector and the government sector must remain separated in this type of credit financing. Mixing these responsibilities such as takes place in West Germany where Anschlussfinanzierung of export credits can be guaranteed by the federal government, or in the United States where the Exim Bank can give long term credits for financing traditional export transactions in the form of development loans, cannot be justified from a commercial viewpoint. Such combinations can only result in an arbitrary credit policy with increasing credit periods. As the private banking sector realizes export credits, the limits which it can cover for its own account and risk are exceeded because of certain consequences inherent in these credits, and the government must offer additional coverage. This creates the danger that commercial principles which should be applied in this type of credit granting cannot be given full justice, because government assistance may result in distorting international competitive conditions in order to conquer export markets by artificial means. These dangers are not evident in boom periods, although they exist, because governments have no reason to follow this course under these circumstances. However, in depression periods such artificial distortions can bring about tremendous dangers because the governments then regard export promotion as a means to solve their unemployment problem. It is therefore necessary to try to reorganize the system during a boom period and to cover risks as much as possible through commercial channels.

We must examine if the role of governments in the commercial sector can be reduced through cooperation in the execution of export credit policies. The arrangements made in the framework of the Bernese Convention, the organization of credit insurers, could be taken as a starting point because these arrangements represent the first breakthrough of individualism in the commercial field. These arrangements consist mainly of restricting time periods in credit insurance contracts whereas information exchanges in the technical field have also taken place.

The problem of commercial export transactions and the role of the government sector in this respect must be studied in a multilateral framework on the basis of experience obtained in the Bernese Union and on the national level. If credits are government insured the restrictions – natural to every non insured credit – regarding the credit periods can be disregarded. A further disturbing factor is that the financing of insured transactions can be supplied in some countries by the central banks against a highly favorable interest rate which distorts the interest rate mechanism. In examining the problems related to commercial export transactions and the role which governments play in this respect, we must recognize that one of the first objectives is to arrive at a unification in conditions of export credit insurance and to decide which transactions are eligible for insurance and which are not. International competition in the field of rates and other conditions can in the long run only result in an unbusinesslike overbidding of these terms. Because the slogan "other governments offer better terms than ours" is voiced in virtually every country, pressures are exerted to offer still more favorable terms beneficial only for the buyer and certainly not for the supplier countries. In addition, it would be in accordance with the prevailing trend to consider these problems not only on a national level, but also on an international one. Experience has been compounded in export credit insurance over a period of fifteen years, though not all in published form. This experience could disclose detailed information in the various risks which exist and the damages resulting from these risks.

In sum, international agreement must therefore be reached on the following aspects:

(1) determination of the limits of the transactions which can be insured;

(2) equalization of the conditions of the insurance;

(3) exchange of information and consequently a crossfertilization of knowledge.

The following remarks can be made with respect to the three risk sectors: bad debt risk, exchange rate risk and political risk.

Bad debt risk

The Swiss and Netherlands examples show that this risk can be covered in the private sector, although only for a limited period of respectively, one and two years, and only when the debtor does not directly or indirectly represent the State. Cooperation between banks and insurance companies might result in an attempt to cover this risk entirely in the private sector preferably not only for a limited period of one or two years but for the whole period. An international agreement such as is being prepared for covering third party liability resulting from the exploitation of nuclear installations could be used as an example. In this agreement the risk is covered to a certain level in the private sector, while the governments individually or collectively only enter into the picture to cover the excess amount. Since a long experience in bad debt insurance is available in contrast to nuclear installations risk insurance, the determination of the risk and the level to be covered in the private sector could be realized through utilizing this experience. A second examination must be made later on to determine whether a still higher proportion of the risk can be covered in the private sector.

Exchange risk

An important evolution has taken place since 1945 in this sector. At that time the currencies of the Western European countries were largely soft currencies. Furthermore, these countries were virtually entirely dependent on their own power. There were two dominating hard currencies, the dollar and the Swiss franc. Now we have a growing number of hard currencies between which a much larger degree of mutual solidarity exists, while the possibility for quick and effective assistance is available through the IMF. There are also now close international links between the governments and the central banks.

Would it not be possible to cover the exchange risk in the private sector through utilizing the experience of the last fifteen years? Assuming that the transaction will not be invoiced in the currency of the debtor country settlements can be made in a number of relatively hard currencies. There will be no problem of course if the invoice is expressed in the currency of the supplier country.

The first installments of the credit can already now be covered in the private sector, while a gradual shifting from the government to the private sector for later periods can be contemplated in the same way as has been described for the bad debt risk.

Political risk

Although experience in various countries such as Switzerland and the Netherlands, has demonstrated that risk can be covered for a longer period on levying a modest premium, it would seem inevitable that the governments continue to play a role in this sector. Only governments can cover this risk in view of the possible volume of this risk that may arise in a certain country or part of the world.

Conclusion

A revision of government credit and guarantee policy on the basis of utilizing available national and international experience for the purpose of shifting as much as possible of the risk coverage to the private sector on a commercial basis deserves serious consideration. On a national basis the governments must endeavour to shift the granting of credits and guarantees in the small business category to the private sector. The governments must also limit their role as much as possible in the category of large government credits or guarantees, while a solution on an international basis must be sought for credits which are too large to be financed locally. As regards export credits, the governments must take the initiative for international cooperation in order to shift the largest possible part of existing risks in this category to the private sector. It will be necessary in this respect to establish in advance which types of credits must be covered in the private sector and which not. Government negotiations could take place in EEC and OEEC or its successor organization, the OECD on the basis of the Bernese Convention agreements.

Competition Between Commercial Banks and Other Financial Institutions

BY DR C. F. KARSTEN
Managing Director Rotterdamsche Bank

I have chosen this subject because it personally fascinates me, but that – of course – is not a sufficient reason for such a choice. I think that it should interest every banker. It is, however, surprising that so few articles are to be found in the banking magazines which treat this problem. Now maybe you will be of the opinion that the competition *between* the commercial banks themselves is more important and should be discussed first. I cannot, however, agree with you on this point. In the first place competition *between* commercial bankers is an important subject for each banker individually but not so much for all bankers together. In most countries of the world the commercial banks have found their place and their daily business is either regulated by special laws or by strong traditions or *even* by both.

The great movement of concentration in the field of commercial banking, which started in the first decades of this century and which had as a result the creation of the big deposit-banks with many branches, has nearly been completed in many of the developed countries – with the exception of the U.S.A. where law and tradition have prevented a nation-wide banking system. Therefore we see in most of the West European countries, and in many countries in other parts of the world as well, a pattern which is formed by three to six or seven big banks together sharing 80 – 90% of the business and a number of smaller institutions, often private or local banks sharing the rest.

If a bank wants to grow bigger than its competitors and it wants to do it quickly it is hardly possible that it can do so by following the traditional lines. In the existing field of operation all banks are more or less of the same efficiency and on top of it there is – still (?) – a certain bond between the bank and its clients which cannot be easily broken. A more aggressive bank can try to woe away some clients of the other banks by quoting better rates or giving some more liberal credit lines, but this method will never bring quick results, not in the last place because the other banks will soon enough fight back.

The situation becomes, however, a different one if the more aggressive bank leaves the traditional paths and starts by giving new services to its clients. By doing so it offers a more overall service to its clients and if this break away from the traditions is not followed quickly by the other banks – which are more often than not hesitant either because they do not see the importance of the new service or because they do not think it in line with their traditional business – then the result will be that this bank will get its contacts with many of the clients of other banks.

The services now rendered by this bank are, however, only new in the sense that they were not offered before by commercial banks. In most cases, however, other financial institutions did give them and go on giving them. *So we see that the competition between the commercial banks leads to competition with other financial institutions.*

In other words the problem we treat to-day is the problem of the ever changing structure of banking and therefore alone it is worthy to be the subject of one of the lectures at this school.

I am well aware that I have been simplifying my case and I am afraid that I will have to go on doing this during my lecture.

There are many more cases of competition between commercial banks and other financial institutions of which several have nothing to do with the "aggressiveness" of one of the commercial banks – some even are the result of aggressiveness of *another* financial institute – but to make things even more difficult the structure of banking, its function in the economy and the position of other financial institutions differ from one country to another so that it is impossible to deal with the subject in general. What I have done so far, however, is to show you – by showing one aspect – how actual the problem is.

What now is the problem?

So far I have talked in more or less general terms without exactly stating *what* the real problem is. I will now try to do this, but I warn you that this is not very easy and that from time to time I have to simplify or state the facts somewhat arbitrarily if we do not want to get lost in the "maze" of all financial institutions.

The explanation for this is in the first place that – I said this earlier – the situation is different from country to country. Now most of you present here are representatives of private banks and as such we rather welcome competition as a healthy thing. And for those who represent some state-owned branch banks – as in France or Italy – they know that the competition between the various state-owned banks is often as fierce as it was at the time that they were privately owned. Competition as such can therefore hardly be the subject of a treatise. It only interests us where it becomes unhealthy as it is falsified by artificial factors such as laws, propaganda or cartels. With unhealthy I mean to say that these factors change the face of competition in such a way that it becomes onerous for some of the competitors so that they are hampered in the fulfilling of their economic task.

The second side of the problem is that we have to state more clearly what we understand by the term "commercial banks." Although there is definitely a difference from country to country you will most probably agree with me that by speaking of commercial banks we mean in the first place such financial institutions which accept deposits, act as an intermediary in the payment traffic and grant loans (whatever their type may be). On the money creating aspect of this I will treat in connection with the role of the bank in monetary policy.

On top of these primal functions most commercial banks in various countries have some other activities, more or less connected with the essential functions.

Now we come to the last part of the title the "other financial" institutions. This is the most difficult to define. I am afraid that we will have to do with a summing-up rather than with a definition. There are at one end banks having very much the same activities as the commercial banks but mainly in a somewhat different field, such as the cooperative agricultural banks. Then the giro-systems, being intermediaries in the money traffic and giving credits or making investments.

There are the specialised institutions, banks of the so-called second category – not creators of money – hirepurchase companies, mortgage banks, savings-banks etc. And there are at the other end a number of institutions for whom the activities in the pure financial field are of secondary importance, the life insurance companies, the pension funds, but also *the financial departments of the big industrial concerns!*

Now having more or less defined the three parts of our subject you will agree with me that we have accepted a Hercules task. The field is too big and we have to limit ourselves to certain aspects of it.

The role of the commercial bank in monetary policy

In my definition of a commercial bank I have only mentioned in passing the ability of such banks to "create" money. I will, however, now go somewhat deeper into this aspect as it leads to a very special position of the commercial banks in the economy of each country, while *this* special position sometimes plays a big role in the competition with other financial institutions. As a matter of fact it is even so that nowadays the commercial banks are in most countries the most important source of money, more important than the original sources, the states and the central banks. This of course has as direct consequence that the role of the banks within the realm of the monetary policy is a very important one. The control of the volume and the price of money is still the major object of central bank policy. For that reason the banks have to accept that restrictions are put on their earning capacity. Most bankers, however, understand that this has to be accepted if only because they can only flourish in a sphere of a sound monetary policy. The situation becomes rather different, however, if the restrictions are so far reaching and only affecting the banks under the control of the central bank that the business community is driven in the hands of the other financial institutions. We have seen such a case in recent years in the U.K. where the alternative liberalization and restriction upon bank credit have induced industry to by-pass the banks and seek their loans elsewhere. If such a movement would gain momentum the effectiveness of the economic role of the banks and so the effectiveness of monetary control would be endangered. I did not say that this is already the case in the U.K. but the danger is there.

A second case where banks are of the opinion that they are unjustly discriminated against is in the U.S.A. with respect to regulation Q. I believe that practically no commercial banker in the U.S. agrees very much with this restriction. The First National City Bank calls it in the April-issue of its Monthly Letter the "most Questionable of all regulations." It provides limits of 1, 2, $2\frac{1}{2}$ and 3% on the rates of interest member banks of the Federal Reserve System are allowed to pay on time and savings accounts. Thus it denies to banks freedom to compete with interest-bearing accounts and to share, as fully as they can afford, the benefit of higher interest earnings with depositors. All this, while shortly before the passage of the legislation in the Thirties, which brought the Regulation into being, the Federal Reserve Board itself had declared that "it is undesirable to further regulate by law the rates of interest which may be paid on deposits, especially since to do so would place member banks at a disadvantage in competition with nonmember banks." Regulation Q gives no doubt an unfair competitive advantage to other financial institutions – savings and loan associations, mutual savings banks and credit unions. Also security dealers enter the banking business by solliciting and accepting what are in effect collateralized interest-bearing deposits by the method of selling securities from their investment inventory with an agreement to buy back at a future date. So, Regulation Q singles out for competitive disadvantage the commercial banks which are the most important credit source for business and – for smaller business – often the only source. No other type of financial institution is subject to legal reserve requirements and to such constant changes in ability to lend and invest to actions of the Federal Reserve Authorities as the commercial banks.

On top of that the sharp rise in income tax rates of the past twenty years has resulted in an enormous increase in taxes paid by the commercial banks. Mutual thrift and lending institutions, have not been similarly burdened.

But bankers in many other countries also have good reason to complain about "artificial influences."

In England the convential cash ratio of 8 per cent to total deposits and the overall liquidity ratio (cash, call loans and Treasury Bills) of at least 30 percent, of the Clearing Banks have lately been stiffened by the calls for special deposits, which are not eligible for inclusion amongst liquid assets. These ratios of liquidity and the special deposits do not apply to other financial institutions, including the Foreign and Overseas Banks, the Merchant Banks, Acceptance and Discount Houses as well as the Finance of Hire Purchase Companies. This is especially remarkable as also the Radcliffe Committee drew the attention to this discrimination, stating: "If ..... it should appear desirable to reinforce the authorities' power by raising the minimum liquidity ratios of the banks appreciably above their present levels, the practicability of imposing comparable restraints to other groups of financial institutions should be considered......

Important groups to be considered for some comparable restraints would be the Building Societies, the Hire Purchase Finance Companies, and probably the Life Insurance Companies."

Competition with state-owned institutions

Another case I want to bring to your attention is the competition between the commercial banks and some state-owned institutions and well in particular the postal giro systems or the postal savingsbanks. A recent example is the struggle between the commercial banks in Sweden and the postal giro system. For a long time the commercial banks had the virtual monopoly in the field of the payments traffic. Since the 1920's, however, the Postgiro System has become more and more popular. It offers a very cheap service through the network of postoffices. As a result of this competition the cheque account has gradually lost its importance and at the end of 1959 accounted for only 14% of the banks total deposits. As late as in 1949 this proportion was still 22%.

In order to meet the competition of the "Postgiro" the commercial banks decided towards the end of 1958 to improve their cheque service by introducing a common "Bankgiro" system similar to the "Postgiro." The administration of the "Postgiro" immediately responded by announcing that their customers would be paid interest on holdings exceeding 50.000 Kr. if they are at least in the account for 14 days. The interest rate offered was fixed as high as 4¼%.

The commercial banks could not, of course, remain passive

after such a measure. They were forced to offer their customers the same interest rate on the same conditions as those offered by the "Postgiro." It is too early to say anything definite about the profitability of the whole "Giro" business, but taking into account the heavy administration costs involved one has reason to doubt if the funds acquired through the system give any profit at all. For the "postgiro" which is operating with state funds and, among other things, has not the same burden of fixed office costs the question of profitability is not as relevant as for the commercial banks.

The reason for quoting this example at length is that I want to emphasize that such a "falsified" competition may endanger on the long run the very existence of the banks. The functioning of acting as a payment intermediary is the basis for their other function and if this is gradually taken away from them, their other functions will suffer. Now you may remark that it is nothing new that some institutions lose their economic function because others are doing it cheaper or better. Well I know that this is true but it has not been proved that the postgiro does it really cheaper or better and it is even less proved that it will be able to fulfil the other function at all.

Competition on an idealistic basis

I have hesitated what title I should give to this example and you may think that I have chosen a wrong one. Ideals and idealism may seem far from the materialistic business of the banks. You may be right but not everybody thinks so. Time and again people stand up and claim that a bank should be established for their particular trade, as the existing banks are not giving the right credits to that particular trade or are making too much profit. Usually the time has learnt that they were wrong and that it was not such a good idea altogether, but there are examples of successes. One of such successes has been in some countries the cooperative farmersbanks (Raiffeisen). They have certainly done a good job and it has to be admitted that their territory was too long neglected by the banks. So far so good. Rather different became it, however, as these banks began to expand and serve non-farmers customers. Again as such I have nothing to say against such a trend, let they serve the public who serve them best.

But then this competition must be on equal terms and the terms here are not equal. These agricultural banks in an earlier stage, definitely fulfilling a social task by assisting the farmers, got in some countries fiscal and sometimes monetary facilities. These facilities, however, are now used as the basis of the extension of business which means that the saying that the law is the same for everybody is no longer true.

Changing patterns in the financial field

It may appear to some of you that by the very choice of my cases I give a one-sided view on the situation. With one exception all my examples have been cases of restricted competition and then where the commercial banks were the suffering party.

It is far from me to try to make you believe that this is the true cross-current of the situation. Of course there are many cases of fair competition with other financial institutions where each competitor has to live by his own wits and only the strongest will win. There are also cases where the commercial banks are in a favoured position either because the competing institutions are limited in their activities by law or statutory rules or because the commercial banks have easier access to the perspective clients because of the other services they render.

Recently we have had such a case in Holland, where the commercial banks, for more than one reason (a.o. in order to be able to compete with the cooperative agriculture banks) have entered the field of the savings-banks. The traditional savings-banks, mostly because of their statutory rules, must limit themselves to non risk bearing investments, with low yields. They claim that the commercial banks, which have not such a limitation, can pay more interest on the savings accounts as they can do. As the commercial banks, however, only seek to attract the bigger savings accounts they leave the savings-banks the unrewarding costly small accounts, which makes it even more difficult for them to make both ends meet. Without giving a judgement on this question it will be understood that we have to deal here not only with an economic but also with a social problem.

But as I said earlier one has to make a choice in this vast field and I wanted to draw your attention to some aspects which do not always seem clear.

Before ending my lecture, however, I would like to show some other aspects of the ever changing frontier in the field of competition between the commercial banks and the other financial institutions. I will limit myself, however, – as I have already used too much of your time – to pointing out some major trends.

(a) Despecialisation

In the beginning of this lecture I told you that the commercial banks – where allowed by the law – broaden the sphere of their activities, thereby strongly competing with specialised institutions. I did already mention savings accounts but I would add medium term credits, hirepurchase credits, trustee departments, etc. This is partly due to the fact that the economic life becomes so integrated that if a commercial bank does not render certain services to its clients it will lose its clients to another institution which does have these departments. *The competition between the commercial banks themselves forces them to compete with other institutions!*

Partly it is due to the changing insight in the theory of banking. The more it is understood that a good part of the bank deposits have to have a stable character, that is to say that as long as a bank will hold its place in the row of banks, it can reckon with a certain portion of money available to it. Understanding this the commercial banks – and the U.S. banks have been leading the way here – started by giving medium term loans. Some people deplore this despecialisation very much but I think that such an attitude does not help very much. Either the banks can give these services better or cheaper or the new departments will not be much of a success. Only in those cases where the banks are only willing to whip off the cream and leave the specialised institutions with the dry bread and skim-milk there might be a reason to intervene. I doubt, however, whether many of such cases do exist. If we see the example of the banks in the U.S.A. it is clear that they develop themselves to real "department stores" giving *every* service.

(b) The institutional investor and the industrial concerns

The banks are, however, not the only lions of the wilderness, two other important sorts of institutions do more and more compete and by their size alone they become mighty competitors.

These competitors are the institutional investors on the one hand and the financial departments of the big industrial concerns on the other hand.

The institutional investors – life insurance companies and great pensionfunds – have grown enormously in importance since World War II often favoured by a good fiscal climate.

But not only have they grown in size they have also changed their investment portfolio, which now partly is made up by shares in industrial companies, loans to such companies and sometimes even short term advances (3-6 months). As the loans so given are more often than not combined with an insurancepolicy the rates are sometimes cut very fine as it is all a package deal. Although the banks lose some business this way I believe that for the time being the specialized institutions (mortgage banks etc.) are the great losers.

More important for the banks is the concentration of industry into big industrial concerns often with a world wide activity. Efficiency alone makes it necessary for these concerns to have a well integrated financial department, which acts among others as a clearinghouse for the liquidities within the concern. Sometimes these departments develop into life size banks (Germany) but even if it is not the case they will take over some of the business formerly done by the banks. For that reason the accounts of such concerns become more a prestige factor for a bank than a direct source of income. Even the largest bank in the world, however, can hardly compete in size with these concerns and it is therefore understandable that they had to go this way.

Conclusions

There is much more I could say but I am afraid that I have already been talking too long.

I have tried, however, to show you what is going on in the financial world and I hope that I have succeeded in showing you that this world is far from rigid. On the contrary I have the feeling that the face of banking has changed very much in the last ten years and will change even more in the next. Banking has long been a traditional trade but now it nearly becomes a revolutionary one. We must not forget that it is mainly due to the fact that competition *has* been possible. There where the banks and the other institutions are strictly regulated by law in their activities much less progress has been made.

The only thing, however, the monetary authorities have to prevent is that competition becomes such that it affects the soundness of the commercial banks (and of the other institutions as well) so that the soundness of the currency becomes endangered. Then they would be forced to take measures.

Although I have hinted at some of these possibilities I do not think that we should exaggerate these dangers.

GPSR Compliance

The European Union's (EU) General Product Safety Regulation (GPSR) is a set of rules that requires consumer products to be safe and our obligations to ensure this.

If you have any concerns about our products, you can contact us on ProductSafety@springernature.com

In case Publisher is established outside the EU, the EU authorized representative is:

Springer Nature Customer Service Center GmbH
Europaplatz 3
69115 Heidelberg, Germany

Batch number: 10823817

Printed by Printforce, the Netherlands